THE WESTERN FRONTIER LIBRARY

WASHINGTON IRVING

A Tour
on the Prairies

WASHINGTON IRVING

A Tour
on the Prairies

Edited with an Introductory Essay

by John Francis McDermott

UNIVERSITY OF OKLAHOMA PRESS: NORMAN

Books Edited and Written by John Francis McDermott
Published by the University of Oklahoma Press

George Caleb Bingham: River Portraitist, 1959
Seth Eastman: Pictorial Historian of the Indian, 1961
Editor of *Tixier's Travels on the Osage Prairies*
(translated by Albert J. Salvan), 1940
Editor of *The Western Journals of Washington Irving,* 1944
Editor of *Up the Missouri with Audubon: The Journal of
Edward Harris,* 1951
Editor of *Indian Sketches,* by John Treat Irving, 1955
Editor of *A Tour on the Prairies,* by Washington Irving, 1956
Editor of *Prairie and Mountain Sketches,* by Matthew C. Field
(collected by Clyde and Mae Reed Porter) (ed. with
Kate L. Gregg), 1957

Cataloging in Publication Data

Irving, Washington, 1783–1859.
A tour on the prairies. Edited with an introductory essay by John
Francis McDermott. Norman, University of Oklahoma Press [1956]

(The Western frontier library [7])

1. Oklahoma—Descr. & trav. 2. Indians of North America—
Oklahoma. I. Title.
F697.I 743   1956   917.66   56–11232
Library of Congress   [10]
ISBN: 0–8061–1958–6

Library of Congress Catalog Card Number: 56–11232

FOR "TIA"

Elizabeth Irwin Elder

Contents

Contents

Foreword

BY RICHARD BATMAN

Washington Irving's *A Tour on the Prairies* came about, at least in part, because of a happy series of accidental meetings. In the spring of 1832, Irving left Europe to return to the United States on the packet ship *Havre*, and while on board, met the Englishman Charles Latrobe and his Swiss traveling companion, Count Albert-Alexandre de Pourtales. A friendship developed, and after reaching the United States, the three men made several excursions together. At first these trips were confined mainly to the East—to West Point, to the Catskills and the land of Sleepy Hollow, to the White Mountains, to Saratoga Springs, and finally to Niagara Falls. It was on this last trip that another accidental meeting sent the three travelers off to see the West and Indian country.

After visiting the falls, the three travelers went to Buffalo, where they boarded a Lake Erie steamer bound for Detroit. At first Irving planned to leave it at some intermediate port and return east alone by way of the Ohio River. But while on board the steamboat, he met Henry Leavitt Ellsworth, who had recently been appointed an Indian commissioner. Ellsworth was on his way to investigate problems among the tribes in Oklahoma, and he invited Irving, Latrobe, and Pourtales to accompany him. They jumped at the chance, and by early September, Irving, instead of being on his way home, was in the river port of Cincinnati, preparing to go west.

Yet if the specific trip was the result of accidental meetings, Irving's decision to see America, to reacquaint himself with it, and to write of it, was also a natural result of the situation in which he found himself upon his return from Europe. He was forty-nine years old, and when he arrived in New York in May, 1832, he had been absent from his native country for the past seventeen years. Like his own creation Rip Van Winkle, he found himself in a much different world from the one he had left behind when he went to Europe in 1815.

During the time that Irving had spent in Europe, he had become one of America's most popular writers, but in recent years he had been aware of a growing coolness on the part of his American audience. He had become thoroughly Europeanized, and he had written mainly of England, of Germany, and most recently, of Spain and the Alhambra. This had created a certain suspicion—or at least indifference —on the part of many readers, and Irving had long been sensitive to this criticism. In fact, like many long-time expatriates, he may well have felt the absence of his homeland and its influence on his work more severely than his critics. Thus, when he returned to America in 1832, he seemed determined to see as much of his native country as possible and to sink roots once again into its soil.

No wonder then that Irving, after meeting Ellsworth, was willing to change his plans on the spur of the moment and accompany him west. Already, while traveling with Latrobe and Pourtales, he had renewed his acquaintance with the eastern part of the country. Now he had the opportunity to fulfill a long-time dream and visit the frontier.

The travelers left Cincinnati on September 3 and the following day were in Louisville. From there they continued on down the Ohio River, then up the Mississippi, until they reached St. Louis on September 13. Here Irving saw many remnants of the early West, as he met Pierre Chouteau, who as a child had been present at the founding of St. Louis in 1764; saw the home on top of an Indian mound that General William Ashley had built with his fur trade profits; and drove out to visit General William Clark in his home stuffed with Indian artifacts. Then, on the following day Irving and his companions went to see the recently captured Indian, Black Hawk, and his followers, all of whom were being held in chains at the military post at Jefferson Barracks. After that the party divided, with Ellsworth going up the Missouri River by steamboat while Irving, Latrobe, and Pourtales crossed the state of Missouri on horseback. At Independence they were reunited, and from there the four men proceeded to Fort Gibson, the departure point for the actual tour of the prairies.

The travelers arrived at Fort Gibson on October 8, only to find that a band of frontier rangers, commanded by Captain Jesse Bean, had been sent West to show the flag among the Indians just two days before. The post commander, Colonel Matthew Arbuckle, immediately sent a message to Bean ordering him to halt and wait until Commissioner Ellsworth and his party could join them. Five days later Ellsworth, Irving, and the others reached the rangers camp. For the rest of October and early November, Irving traveled with them through Indian country, ascending the Cimarron River almost as far as what is today Guthrie, Oklahoma, then angling west and south through the Cross Timbers, reaching the Little River near Norman. Then the party turned east and arrived back at Fort Gibson on November 9.

Throughout the entire trip, Irving kept a journal, and soon after his return east he began to convert the entries into a narrative of his western trip.[1] There were many dis-

---

[1] Washington Irving, *The Western Journals* (Norman: University of Oklahoma Press, 1944), p. 10.

tractions, however; and it was not until November, 1834, that he finally finished it. In March, 1835, *A Tour on the Prairies* was published in London, and the following month Carey, Lee, and Blanchard brought out the American edition.

A Tour on the Prairies—Irving's first published work since his return to the United States—is in many ways a watershed in his writing career. He had become accustomed to thinking and writing in terms easily identified in Europeanized circles, a habit he found difficult to break. A rock formation looks like "the ruin of some Moorish castle," and sunlight in the forest reminds him of "the effect of sunshine among the stained windows and clustering columns of a Gothic cathedral." The same is true of men met along the way. An Osage Indian has "a fine Roman countenance," a lean frontiersman reminds him of "the hero of La Mancha," while Tonish, cast in the role of comic servant, is "a Gil Blas of the frontier."

Yet in spite of the sometimes-too-easy references to European themes, a real feel for the western country and its inhabitants, Indian and white, comes through in *A Tour on the Prairies.* If, at first glance, the ranger's camp is described as a "wild bandit, or Robin Hood, scene," the hard life of frontier military men is later thoroughly and accurately portrayed. If Old Ryan, the hunter, is too quickly characterized as "the Nestor of our camp," he, too, is developed as a thoroughly western type. On the surface Irving is still seriously influenced—his critics would say damaged—by all those years in Europe; but just beneath that surface, it is clear that his tour on the prairies has reintroduced him to his native America, and to themes he had ignored for years.

The West opened new subjects for Irving. Ten years earlier, while living in Paris, he had met John Jacob Astor, and upon returning to America, he had renewed the acquaintance. Even before *A Tour on the Prairies* was published,

Foreword

Irving had agreed to write a history of Astor's attempt to open the American fur trade on the Pacific Coast. The popularity of *A Tour on the Prairies* only strengthened the decision to write of the West, and out of it, of course, came Washington Irving's *Astoria,* which was followed later by his *Adventures of Captain Bonneville.*

Editor's Preface

T HE LAST PIECE of work I completed before entering
the service in 1942 was an edition of *The Western Journals
of Washington Irving*. Rediscovering Irving's notebooks
(they had been published with others more than twenty
years earlier in a very small edition and had been long out
of print) in the course of other work on the frontier, I
thought them, even though incomplete, among the most
valuable and fascinating firsthand accounts of the early
West. I think so still. But in my enthusiasm for these journals as documents, I spoke disparagingly of *A Tour on the
Prairies*, and, I now believe, without full understanding of
the author's purpose and point of view or the value of the
book as an art record. My chief objection, as I look back,
was that Irving had not written the book I then wanted
from him. An author, however, is to be judged on what he
proposed and accomplished, not on what the reader or
critic preferred to have him do.

A suggestion several years ago that I edit the *Tour* led
me to a careful reconsideration of it. Certainly some part
of what I said in my introduction to the *Western Journals*
(pages 40–62) is still valid: biographically, the presentation
of Tonish and Beatte is unfair. I maintain, too, that some
passages in the *Tour* are sentimental and "literary." Such
faults, however, are to be found in the work of any prolific
artist. But I have discovered a great deal that is excellent
in the book Irving published, and I think I have come on
the very open secret of its early acceptance and its constant

interest: a point of view which Irving's critics hitherto have not realized, though he underscored it in his pen name, Geoffrey Crayon. Irving was an artist with the pencil (as the phrase was in his day) who substituted the word for the stroke of the crayon and the brush. It was my work, over the years since the war, in American art history—particularly American genre—that led me to understand and value Irving as genre painter. How true that is of the *Tour* I show in the introduction that follows.

The present edition is based on the author's edition of 1859. I have permitted myself only the slightest changes in punctuation occasionally when clarity demanded. That Irving might be allowed full expression of his personal point of view I have added the original author's introduction to the American edition of 1835.

My work with Irving has extended over so many years that it is difficult to recall my debts and obligations. But I can renew my thanks to the persons and institutions that supplied me with information and aid in the preparation of the *Western Journals*, for I have sometimes drawn on those sources here. I never complete any research project without real indebtedness to the library of Washington University, to the Missouri Historical Society, and to the St. Louis Mercantile Library for courtesies beyond the call of duty. My friend Frederic E. Voelker was kind enough to lend me his first American edition of the *Tour*. Mrs. R. M. Kendrick (my mother-in-law) helped in the cross reading of texts. Others who provided very special help include the late Grant Foreman, of Muskogee, Oklahoma; John C. Ewers, of the Smithsonian Institution; and the staff of the New York Public Library. First and last, of course, now and always, comes Mary Stephanie McDermott, my wife, my typist, and my critic.

St. Louis   JOHN FRANCIS MCDERMOTT

Introductory Essay

BY JOHN FRANCIS MCDERMOTT

I

A Tour on the Prairies is first of all a voyage of personal discovery. Washington Irving's excursion into the wild lands beyond the frontier was not a pathfinding exploration such as Lewis and Clark made, nor a business enterprise such as Wilson Price Hunt or Josiah Gregg undertook, nor a military survey like that of Frémont, nor a search for beasts or birds or plants like Bradbury's or Nuttall's or Audubon's. Irving's was a voyage of discovery made by a man who had been long absent from his home and who wanted now to see and feel and smell and hear his own country, who ardently desired to realize it for himself. His book was the personal record of "a month's foray beyond the outposts of human habitation . . . a simple narrative of every day occurrences; such as happen to every one who travels the prairies." He had "no wonders to describe, nor any moving accidents by flood or field to narrate;"—and story, "none to tell, sir."[1]

Out of a brief round over the Oklahoma prairies, on a military mission of no importance, during which the party saw not one hostile Indian, nor gathered any significant information about terrain, nor marked a road, nor accomplished anything except to wear out a few horses and to run short of food—out of this unpromising material Washington Irving made a travel book that was immediately

[1] Author's Introduction. All quotations not otherwise acknowledged are from *A Tour on the Prairies*, as reprinted here.

taken up by the reading public, as Stanley T. Williams, his chief biographer, has remarked with some astonishment, even though it was "unscientific [and] unenriched by new data."[2] Its perennial popularity owes much to the suavity, the urbanity, the geniality, the grace of expression which his critics have commonly allowed Irving, for the man could write as few of his contemporaries could. But the book is more than a literary exercise. Its true worth and its enduring fascination lie in the brilliantly drawn pictures of frontier life that flow from the pencil of a great genre artist.

It was a chance meeting on a Lake Erie steamboat late in August, 1832, that sent Irving southwest over the prairies.[3] Returning from a seventeen-year residence in Eu-

[2] *The Life of Washington Irving* (New York, Oxford University Press, 1935), II, 80–81.

[3] Irving had left New York early in August for Saratoga, where he met once more his traveling friends Latrobe and Pourtalès. With them he visited Trenton Springs not far from Utica and then Niagara Falls. At Buffalo, New York, they boarded a steamer for Detroit, the Europeans intending to return by way of Montreal and Quebec, Irving proposing to cross Ohio and thence home by river. But they met Henry Leavitt Ellsworth on the boat. "After some acquaintance we discoursed upon the nature of my mission [Ellsworth wrote from Fort Gibson, December 5, 1832], and discovering a desire to accompany me, I invited them all to go with me even to the Buffalo range, promising them the protection of the Government, and my individual exertions to make their excursion pleasant." (Stanley T. Williams and Barbara D. Simison, "A Journey through Oklahoma in 1832: A Letter from Henry L. Ellsworth to Professor Benjamin Silliman," *Mississippi Valley Historical Review*, Vol. XXIX, No. 3 [December, 1942], 387–93.) The four travelers reached Cincinnati on September 1, St. Louis on September 13, and Fort Gibson on October 8. For a full account of Irving's western travels, of Ellsworth's mission, and of Captain Bean's Rangers, see *The Western Journals of Washington Irving*, edited by John Francis McDermott (Norman, University of Oklahoma Press, 1944), 3–40.

rope, eager to know what his native land had become, he was ripe for a suggestion which would open new vistas in his life. When Henry L. Ellsworth, newly-appointed commissioner to treat with the western Indians, invited him to go out to Fort Gibson as secretary *pro tem* to the commission, Irving fired up with enthusiasm. "The offer was too tempting to be resisted," he wrote to his brother Peter. "I should have an opportunity of seeing the remnants of those great Indian Tribes, which are now about to disappear as independent nations, or to be amalgamated under some new form of government. I should see those fine countries of the 'far west,' while still in a state of pristine wildness, and behold herds of buffaloes scouring their native prairies, before they are driven beyond the reach of a civilized tourist."[4]

Putting aside other plans, Irving and his traveling companions Latrobe and Pourtalès landed with Ellsworth at Ashtabula, crossed Ohio to Cincinnati, passed by steamboat to St. Louis, and thence by horseback via Independence to the Arkansas. Arrived at the southwestern outpost, Fort Gibson, Irving felt he was now "completely launched in savage life" and was "extremely excited and interested by this wild country, and the wild scenes and people" by which he was surrounded.[5] He was delighted to set out with Ellsworth and a company of Rangers on a foray "beyond human habitation." His notebooks, his letters, his narrative repeatedly display his eager participation in the new life. The expedition reaching the Red

[4] Washington City, December 18, 1832. Originally published in the London *Athenaeum* (1833), 137–38; reprinted in the New York *Commercial Advertiser*, and copied from the latter by the *Arkansas Gazette*, June 26, 1833.

[5] Irving to his sister, Mrs. Paris; Fort Gibson, October 9, 1832. Pierre M. Irving, *The Life and Letters of Washington Irving* (4 vols., London, Richard Bentley, 1862–64), III, 23.

Fork of the Arkansas (the Cimarron), a stream too broad
and deep for fording, Irving was charmingly pleased by
the boat their man Beatte constructed from a buffalo hide.
When it had been half filled with saddles, saddlebags, and
other luggage and placed in the water, Irving stepped in
"as cautiously as possible, and sat down on the top of the
luggage, the margin of the hide sinking to within a hand's
breadth of the water's edge. Rifles, fowling-pieces, and
other articles of small bulk, were then handed in, until I
protested against receiving any more freight. We then
launched forth upon the stream, the bark being towed as
before. It was with a sensation half serious, half comic, that
I found myself thus afloat, on the skin of a buffalo, in the
midst of a wild river, surrounded by wilderness, and towed
along by a half savage, whooping and yelling like a devil
incarnate."

In camp the next day, having traveled by this time more
than one hundred miles from Fort Gibson, he summed up
in his journal the pleasures and satisfactions of his excursion:

Delightful mode of life—exercise on horseback all the fore
part of the day—diversified by hunting incidents—then
about 3 oclock encamping in some beautiful place with
full appetite for repose, lying on the grass under green
trees—in genial weather with a blue, cloudless sky—then
so sweet sleeping at night in the open air, & when awake
seeing the moon and stars through the tree tops—such zest
for the hardy, simple, but savory meats, the product of
the chase—venison roasted on spits or broiled on the coals
—turkeys just from the thicket—honey from the tree—
coffee—or delightful prairie tea. The weather is in its perfection—golden sunshine—not oppressive but animating—
skies without a cloud—or if there be clouds, of feathery

texture and lovely tints—air pure, bland, exhilarating—an
atmosphere of perfect transparency—and the whole country having the mellow tint of autumn. How exciting to
think that we are breaking thro a country hitherto untrodden by white man, except perchance the solitary trapper—a glorious world spread around us without an inhabitant.[6]

In *A Tour on the Prairies*, then, we have the zestful
response of a man to his first experience beyond the Western Frontier. But Irving has a great deal more to offer
than a readable account of personal experience. His book
is a document, for in it he has preserved a segment of society. Its scenes and activities are original and unique because, perceiving them as an artist, he captured life rather
than merely recorded information. The historian searching for facts who finds none in the *Tour* is gravely limited
in his concept of the word. Facts are not limited to scientific, military, topographical, ethnological, or commercial data: whatever "fixes" a scene of human activity or a
person is a fact. Irving's intention, as much as his skill,
differs from that of other travelers. He had no scientific
training or interest; consequently, he gathered no scientific
information. He was not a soldier or a pathfinder or a
businessman and did not concern himself with the affairs
of such persons. He was, in his own word, a tourist—a
visitor traveling for his own information, seeking to find
out for himself what this frontier country and its people
were like. He had no purpose but to observe human behavior. He made his own discoveries—and these discoveries
are facts as valuable in the long run as the finding of an
undescribed plant or the charting of a river or the locating

[6] October 16; *The Western Journals of Washington Irving*, 130–
31. This work will hereafter be referred to as *Western Journals*.

of a new pass through the mountains. Any intelligent traveler may collect information: only an artist of true skill can capture in sketches the living world about him.

The "occurrences that happen to every man who travels the prairies" are set down in the *Tour* with an intimate detail, a sense of values, an understanding of behavior, a pictorial vividness seldom found in the journals of men concerned with scientific or military or commercial purposes. Traveling with Irving, we learn the difficulty of fording deep streams on horseback, of working through mile after mile of tangled undergrowth ("forests of cast iron") like the Cross Timbers. With him we are jogging comfortably on when a thunderstorm breaks and the rain comes "rattling upon us in torrents, and spattered up like steam along the ground; the whole landscape was suddenly wrapped in gloom that gave a vivid effect to the intense sheets of lightning, while the thunder seemed to burst over our very heads, and was reverberated by the groves and forests that checkered and skirted the prairie. Man and beast were so pelted, drenched, and confounded, that the line was thrown in complete confusion; some of the horses were so frightened as to be almost unmanageable, and our scattered cavalcade looked like a tempest-tossed fleet, driven hither and thither, at the mercy of wind and wave."

We see horses worn out and abandoned. We live on the country, and we learn what it is, with our small supply of flour exhausted, to find no game better than a few birds that we scorned when venison and buffalo were aplenty. In the immensity of the prairie we too come to understand that there is "something inexpressibly lonely. . . . The loneliness of a forest seems nothing to it. There the view is shut in by trees, and the imagination is left free to picture some livelier scene beyond. But here we have an immense extent of landscape without a sign of human exist-

ence. We have the consciousness of being far, far beyond
the bounds of human habitation; we feel as if moving in
the midst of a desert world. . . . The silence of the waste
. . . now and then broken by the cry of a distant flock
of pelicans, stalking like spectres about a shallow pool . . .
the sinister croaking of a raven in the air . . . [a wolf whin-
ing] with tones that gave a dreariness to the surrounding
solitude."

Nowhere else do we get to know a military company
as we do these Rangers. Irving was not an army officer to
be concerned with the effectiveness of his unit or the impression that the world might get of his professional apti-
tude. He was free to "ramble among the natural actions
of men,"[7] and he brought together a lively record of a
most casual and unmilitary outfit, representative enough
of short-term volunteers in that day. A "raw, undisciplined
band, levied among the wild youngsters of the frontier,"
who had signed up "for the sake of roving adventure,"
they were without a tradition of military service, without
training, without uniforms or commissary, without consciousness of rank. "Many of them were the neighbors of
their officers and accustomed to regard them with the fa
miliarity of equals and companions. None of them had any
idea of the restraint and decorum of a camp, or ambition
to acquire a name for exactness in a profession in which
they had no intention of continuing." Restless, rough,
good-natured, adventurous, wasteful, stuffed with curious lore, they possibly did not know that they were sitting for their portrait, but they could not have cared less.

Peals of laughter, ribald jokes, lugubrious psalms, mock-

[7] His own phrase as reported by Ellsworth, *Washington Irving
on the Prairie or a Narrative of a Tour of the Southwest in the Year
1832* (New York, American Book Company, 1937), 71. Ellsworth's
work will hereafter be referred to as *Narrative*.

ery of comrades resounded at the evening campfires. Stories of their hunting adventures, gossip of their neighborhoods, and secondhand tales about the Indians filled the idle hours. The day's ride over the prairie took little out of them: they were at any moment leaping, wrestling, shooting at a mark, indulging in horseplay. One morning, "scarcely had the first gray streak of dawn appeared, when a youngster at one of the distant lodges, shaking off his sleep, crowed in imitation of a cock, with a loud, clear note and prolonged cadence." Another "rooster" answered immediately, and in a moment, "the chant was echoed from lodge to lodge, and followed by the cackling of hens, quacking of ducks, gabbling of turkeys, and grunting of swine."

The Rangers were eternally trading: "In the course of our expedition, there was scarce a horse, rifle, powderhorn, or blanket, that did not change owners several times." Carelessly destructive and appallingly wasteful they were: "our late bustling encampment [Irving wrote one day] had a forlorn and desolate appearance. The surrounding forest had been in many places trampled into a quagmire. Trees felled and partly hewn in pieces, and scattered in huge fragments; tent-poles stripped of their covering; smouldering fires, with great morsels of roasted venison and buffalo meat, standing in wooden spits before them, hacked and slashed by the knives of hungry hunters; while around were strewed the hides, the horns, the antlers and bones of buffaloes and deer, with uncooked joints, and unplucked turkeys, left behind with reckless improvidence and wastefulness which young hunters are apt to indulge when in a neighborhood where game abounds. In the meantime a score or two of turkey-buzzards, or vultures, were already on the wing, wheeling their magnificent flight high in air, and preparing for a descent upon the camp as soon as it should be abandoned."

"The Indian of poetical fiction," Irving underscored, "is like the shepherd of pastoral romance, a mere personification of imaginary attributes." Uninfluenced by personal concerns, Irving found the Indian not the solemn, stoical hero or the sullen vermin that most travelers reported him, but a human being lively and humorous. Repeatedly Irving noticed the "excitability and boisterous merriment" of the Osages at their games and more than once had seen a group "sitting around a fire until a late hour of the night, engaged in the most animated and lively conversation; and at times making the woods resound with peals of laughter."

Taciturn he found the Indians "when in company of white men, whose good-will they distrust, and whose language they do not understand," and so would the white man be, he said, under like circumstances. But among themselves, "there cannot be greater gossips. Half their time is taken up in talking over their adventures in war and hunting, and in telling whimsical stories. They are great mimics and buffoons, also, and entertain themselves excessively at the expense of the whites with whom they have associated, and who have supposed them impressed with profound respect for their grandeur and dignity. They are curious observers, noting every thing in silence, but with a keen and watchful eye; occasionally exchanging a glance or a grunt with each other, when any thing particularly strikes them: but reserving all comments until they are alone. Then it is that they give full scope to criticism, satire, mimicry, and mirth."

On one occasion their skill at improvising was demonstrated for Irving. Three Osages joined their evening campfire and after supper began a chant, which, the interpreter told the tourists, "related to ourselves, our appearance, our treatment of them, and all they knew of our plans. In one part they spoke of the young Count, whose animated character and eagerness for Indian enterprise had struck their fancy, and they indulged in some waggery about him and the young Indian beauties, that produced great merriment among our half-breeds."

Indian humor found expression in other ways. With straight faces the tall Osages (famous as walkers) explained the desperate valor of their once-deadly foes the Delawares: "Look at the Delawares—dey got short leg—no can run—must stand and fight a great heap." There was something too of dry satire in Osage reaction to speeches by the Commissioner. The expedition coming on a village empty of warriors, Mr. Ellsworth seriously called together the women and children and old men and "made a speech from on horseback; informing his hearers of the purport of his mission, to promote a general peace among the tribes of the West, and urging them to lay aside all warlike and bloodthirsty notions, and not to make any wanton attacks upon the Pawnees." The speech, interpreted by Beatte, "seemed to have a most pacifying effect upon the multitude, who promised faithfully that, as far as in them lay, the peace should not be disturbed."

Late in the excursion they met a war party of seven Osage hunters who hoped to carry off some Pawnee scalps or horses before returning to their village. The Commissioner "now remembered his mission as pacificator, and made a speech, exhorting them to abstain from all offensive acts against the Pawnees; informing them of the plan of their father at Washington, to put an end to all war among his red children; and assuring them that he was sent to the frontier to establish a universal peace. He told them, therefore, to return quietly to their homes, with the certainty that the Pawnees would no longer molest them, but would soon regard them as brothers." To such solemn and well-intentioned but somewhat naïve remarks the Indians listened "with their customary silence and decorum; after which, exchanging a few words among themselves, they bade us farewell." Because he fancied he saw a smile lurking on Beatte's face, Irving asked him privately what the Indians had said to each other after the speech. The interpreter replied that the leader had observed that "as their great father intended so soon to put an end to all warfare, it behooved them to make the most of the little time that was left them. So they had departed, with redoubled zeal, to pursue their project of horse-stealing!"

It is not merely in the life he gave to the trials and difficulties and commonplaces of prairie travel or the military informality of the Rangers or his interpretation of Indians as real people that the excellence of the *Tour* lies. Most notable of all is Irving's skill as a genre artist. He had feeling as a landscapist and produced views that would qualify him for the Hudson River school,[8] but his forte was genre, the portrayal of scenes of everyday life, as it had been since his earliest years. The masterful handling of composition and color, the superb drawing, the simplicity and variety of details, the commonplace character yet unique quality of his subjects, the clarity of vision, the unity of tone and the feeling for action, and the objective realism with which he saw life combine to produce a re-

---

[8] Many examples could be cited; I quote a passage at the crossing of the Red Fork: "The river scenery at this place was beautifully diversified, presenting long, shining reaches, bordered by willows and cotton-wood trees; rich bottoms, with lofty forests; among which towered enormous plane trees, and the distance was closed in by high embowered promontories."

markable picture of life in far western America. Few of his fellows of the brush could attain his effects. It is no wonder that he still charms us.

Very early in the narrative we are vividly aware that he saw life with a painter's eye. Eager to begin his tour, Irving rode over from Fort Gibson to Chouteau's post on the Verdigris, from which they were to set out. In the background he saw "a few log houses on the banks of the river." An escort of a dozen rangers was waiting for the Commissioner: some "on horseback, some on foot, some seated on the trunks of fallen trees, some shooting at a mark." A motley crew they were, dressed in "frock-coats made of green blankets . . . [or] leathern hunting-shirts" and "marvellously ill-cut garments, much the worse for wear, and evidently put on for rugged service."

His quick eye moved on to a group of Osages, stately fellows, stern and simple in garb and aspect. No ornaments. Their only dress blankets, leggings, and moccasins. Heads bare, hair cropped close, except for a bristly ridge on the top like the crest of a helmet with a long scalp lock hanging behind. Blankets wrapped about their loins, leaving bust and arms bare—noble bronze figures, the finest looking Indians in the West. In contrast, there was a band of gayly-dressed Creeks "in calico hunting-shirts of various brilliant colors, decorated with bright fringes, and belted with broad girdles, embroidered with beads." Leggings of dressed deerskin or of green and scarlet cloth, embroidered knee bands and tassels. Moccasins fancifully ornamented. Gaudy handkerchiefs around their heads. Elsewhere he saw "a sprinkling of trappers, hunters, half-breeds, creoles, negroes of every hue."

The picture is not yet rich enough. Observe the special studies that fill spaces left in this superb canvas. Movement everywhere. A blacksmith's shed with "a strapping negro

... shoeing a horse" and two half-bloods "fabricating iron spoons in which to melt lead for bullets." Near by, "an old trapper, in leathern hunting frock and moccasons, had placed his rifle against a work-bench, while he superintended the operation, and gossiped about his hunting exploits." Dogs are "lounging in and out of the shop, or sleeping in the sunshine." Watching the horseshoeing is "a little cur, with head cocked to one side, and one ear erect . . . with that curiosity common to little dogs . . . as if studying the art, or waiting his turn to be shod." Here is no prettifying, no seeking of glamor, no indulgence in the mere picturesque, no romantic dreaming about an imaginary world. This is life itself on the frontier. Not until a decade later in George Caleb Bingham does America produce a painter to stand with Irving in the portrayal of western scene and character.

Occasionally Irving slipped into the sentimental, into well-tried literary reference, into mere picture making, but what prolific artist has not? Banditti and Moorish towers and Don Quixote and Gil Blas we could readily do without, but they fill few pages in his abundant portfolio. Rather, it is crowded with vigorous, quickly and surely drawn sketches of American frontier life, the frontiersmen, the Indians, the Rangers. Turn back to the crossing of the Red Fork at the moment when the artist has climbed out of the bullboat. With him we watch the "raft of logs and branches, on which the Captain and his prime companion, the Doctor were ferrying their effects across the stream; and . . . a long line of rangers on horseback, fording the stream obliquely, along a series of sand-bars, about a mile and a half distant."

See the Rangers in camp, all "bustle and repose." Some of the men were "busy round the fires, jerking and roasting venison and bear's meat, to be packed up as a future

supply. Some were stretching and dressing the skins of the
animals they had killed; others were washing their clothes
in the brook, and hanging them on the bushes to dry; while
many were lying on the grass, and lazily gossiping in the
shade. Every now and then a hunter would return, on
horseback or on foot, laden with game, or empty handed.
Those who brought home any spoil, deposited it at the
Captain's fire, and then filed off to their respective messes."

They break camp of a morning: "Horses driven in from
the purlieus of the camp; rangers riding about among
rocks and bushes in quest of others that had strayed to a
distance; the bustle of packing up camp equipage, and the
clamor after kettles and frying-pans borrowed by one
mess from another, mixed up with oaths and exclamations
at restive horses, or others that had wandered away to
graze after being packed." The bugle sounds, and the
troop rides off in irregular file, disappearing through the
open forest. "The rear-guard remained under the trees in
the lower part of the dell, some on horseback, with their
rifles on their shoulders; others seated by the fire or lying
on the ground, gossiping in a low, lazy tone of voice, their
horses unsaddled, standing and dozing around: while one
of the rangers, profiting by this interval of leisure, was
shaving himself before a pocket mirror stuck against the
trunk of a tree."

Look at the portrait-sketches. The young Count, "caracoling his horse, and dashing about in the buoyancy of
youthful spirits," has given himself over completely to
the adventure of the frontier. There he is, clad in "a gay
Indian hunting frock of dressed deer skin, setting well to
the shape, dyed of a beautiful purple, and fancifully embroidered with silks of various colors; as if it had been
the work of some Indian beauty, to decorate a favorite
chief. With this he wore leathern pantaloons and mocca-

sons, a foraging cap, and a double-barrelled gun slung by a bandoleer athwart his back." The perfect frontier dandy.

In contrast, observe Pierre Beatte, man of the frontier, guide and interpreter, "lounging about, in an old hunting frock and metasses or leggings, of deer skin, soiled and greased, and almost japanned by constant use." Perhaps thirty-six years of age, square and strongly build, he had features "not unlike those of Napoleon, but sharpened up, with high Indian cheek bones. Perhaps the dusky greenish hue of his complexion, aided his resemblance to an old bronze bust I had seen of the Emperor. He had, however, a sullen, saturnine expression, set off by a slouched woolen hat, and elf locks that hung about his ears. . . . He was cold and laconic; made no promises or professions; stated the terms he required for the services of himself and his horse, which we thought rather high, but showed no disposition to abate them, nor any anxiety to secure our employ."

One final scene. Weary and hungry, Irving and his horse crept on the last stage of their journey homeward. Suddenly before him was a farmhouse, "a low tenement of logs, overshadowed by great forest trees . . . a stable and barn, and granaries teeming with abundance, while legions of grunting swine, gobbling turkeys, cackling hens and strutting roosters, swarmed about the farm-yard." Irving glanced into the cabin. "There sat the Captain of the Rangers and his officers, round a three-legged table, crowned by a broad and smoking dish of boiled beef and turnips." Irving sprang off his horse. A fat, good-humored negress met him at the door. "In a twinkling, she lugged from the fire a huge iron pot. . . . Placing a brown earthen dish on the floor, she inclined the corpulent cauldron on one side, and out leaped sundry great morsels of beef, with a regiment of turnips tumbling after them, and a rich cascade of broth overflowing the whole. This she handed me with an ivory smile that extended from ear to ear; apologizing for our humble fare, and the humble style in which it was served up. Humble fare! humble style! Boiled beef and turnips, and an earthen dish to eat them from! To think of apologizing for such a treat to a half-starved man from the prairies; and then such magnificent slices of bread and butter!"

In such vivid portrayal of the common life on the frontier is the genius of Irving and the enduring interest of his *Tour on the Prairies*.

II

On his excursion to the West, Irving continued his life-long habit of keeping notebooks. "His mode of recording events," Ellsworth observed, "is not to confide much to the memory, but to sketch in a little book every occurence worthy of remembrance and especially *dates* & *facts*."[9] Although he must have filled at least ten notebooks during those four months, only five are extant. These cover his route from Cincinnati to St. Louis, September 3–14; from Independence, Missouri, to Cabin Creek some seventy miles north of Fort Gibson, September 26–October 6; from Cabin Creek to a point on the Red Fork (Cimarron) reached two days after crossing the Arkansas, October 6–17; from a camp on the Little River to Fort Gibson, October 31–November 10; from Fort Gibson to Stack Island in the Mississippi, about 120 miles below the Arkansas, November 11–17.[10] As far as the *Tour* is concerned, the im-

[9] Ellsworth, *Narrative*, 71.

[10] The extant notebooks are all included in my edition of *Western Journals*, published in 1944 by the University of Oklahoma Press. About eight years ago, however, a journal for the overland travel from Ashtabula to Cincinnati was in the possession of Walter

portant lacuna is the journal covering thirteen days of the
prairie excursion, a portion to which he devoted Chapters XVI–XXXII inclusive in the published account. The
Tour and the *Western Journals* then are complementary,
not identical works.

Although as a professional literary man all was grist to
Irving's mill, he had while traveling no immediate and defi-
nite plans for a book about the West. Public pressure, however, was great. The tour was made, Irving said in his
preface, "for the gratification of my curiosity, [but] it has
been supposed that I did it for the purpose of writing a
book." The newspapers everywhere played up these ex-
pectations. The editor of the Columbia *Missouri Intelli-
gencer*, on September 29, 1832 (he had met the travelers
ten days earlier on their way to the southwest prairies),
declared that Irving "will no doubt acquire a valuable fund
of materials in his progress, for interesting works or
Sketches, which, ere long, we may have the gratification
of perusing."[11] At the close of the tour when Irving arrived in Little Rock, the *Arkansas Gazette* (November
21, 1832) held that "Should he favor the world with a
description [of the prairies] from his glowing pen, which
is more than probable, it will excite emotions of unmingled
delight in the bosom of thousands, and unfold innumerable beauties in nature, which, to the majority of travellers,
remain unnoticed and unknown." The editor of that paper,
on January 30, 1833, commenting on the extensiveness of
Irving's western trip, predicted "the result . . . will be
in every way gratifying. The ardent patriotism of the
author of Columbus will prompt him to inspire his coun-

Hill, an antiquarian bookseller of Chicago; since his death, its where-
abouts remain unknown.

[11] I owe this reference to Floyd C. Shoemaker, secretary of the
State Historical Society of Missouri.

trymen with some of his own laudable curiosity about the
land we live in; and his pen, invigorated by themes so novel
to the rest of the world and so grateful to himself, will
trace his impressions with a freshness and force that will
rival its happiest exercise in any of his works." The New
York *Commercial Advertiser*, early in 1833 (republishing
from the London *Athenaeum* his letter of December 18,
1832, to his brother Peter), earnestly hoped that it would
not be long "before we have something more than a *sketch*
of this interesting tour; although we believe he has as yet
written nothing upon the subject for the press."[12]

Irving had always "had a repugnance, amounting almost
to disability, to write in the face of expectation." Never-
theless, he presently faced the job, "plucked a few leaves"
out of his notebooks, and by November 24, 1834, had completed the narrative of his excursion. A copy of the manu-
script he sent off to Colonel Thomas Aspinwall in London before January 8, 1835, and the English edition was
brought out by Murray in March. On April 11, he was
able to tell Peter, "My 'Tour on the Prairies' has just been
published" in Philadelphia. By November 10, Carey, Lea
and Blanchard's American edition was in its eighth thousand.[13] Since that time the "little narrative" that Irving
let go to press with such hesitancy has passed through more
than thirty editions in English and twenty in translation.[14]
Certainly it is well established as a minor American classic.

[12] See note 4.

[13] Pierre M. Irving, *Life and Letters of Washington Irving*, III,
43–46; Washington Irving to Henry Carey, New York, April 8,
1835 (New York Public Library). Pierre M. Irving said his uncle
received $2,400 in all from American sales and £400 for the English
rights. Williams (*Life of Washington Irving*, II, 74) gives the latter
figure as £600.

[14] Stanley T. Williams and Mary Allen Edge, *A Bibliography of
the Writings of Washington Irving* (New York, Oxford University
Press, 1936).

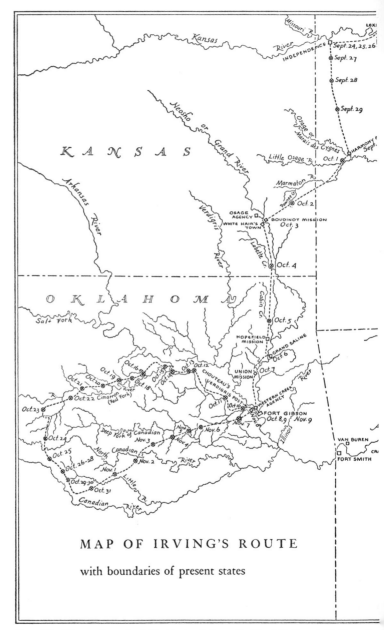

MAP OF IRVING'S ROUTE

with boundaries of present states

From *The Western Journals of Washington Irving*, edited by John Francis McDermott

WASHINGTON IRVING

A Tour
on the Prairies

Author's Introduction[1]

$\mathbb{A}$s I saw the last blue line of my native land fade away, like a cloud in the horizon, it seemed as if I had closed one volume of the world and its concerns, and had time for meditation, before I opened another. That land, too, now vanishing from my view, which contained all that was most dear to me in life; what vicissitudes might occur in it—what changes might take place in me, before I should visit it again! Who can tell, when he sets forth to wander, whither he may be driven by the uncertain currents of existence; or when he may return; or whether it may ever be his lot to revisit the scenes of his childhood!"[2]

Such were the dubious thoughts that passed like a shade across my mind many years since, as I lost sight of my native land, on my voyage to Europe. Yet, I had every reason for bright anticipations. I was buoyant with health, had enough of the "world's gear" for all my wants, was on my way to visit the fairest scenes of Europe, with the prospect of returning home in a couple of years, stored with recollections for the remainder of my life.

The boding doubts, however, which had beclouded my mind at the moment of departure, threatened to prove prophetic. Years and years elapsed, yet I remained a voluntary exile from my home. Why did I so?—The question has often been asked; for once I will make a brief reply.

It was my lot, almost on landing in Europe, to experi-

[1] From the first American edition, 1835.
[2] From "The Voyage," in *The Sketch Book*, 1819.

ence a reverse of fortune, which cast me down in spirit, and altered the whole tenor of my life. In the midst of perplexities and humiliations, I turned to my pen for solace and support. I had hitherto exercised it for amusement; I now looked to it as my main dependence, resolving, if successful, never to abandon it for any prospect of worldly gain, nor to return to my friends, until, by my literary exertions, I had placed myself above their pity, or assistance.

Such are the main reasons that unexpectedly beguiled me into a long protracted absence. How and why that absence was thus protracted, would involve a story of baffled plans and deferred hopes, which led me on from month to month, and year to year, and left me where they found me; would involve, in short, the checquered story of my humble concerns and precarious feelings—and I have a shrinking repugnance to such an exposure.

Suffice it to say, that my path, which many are apt to think was a flowery one, was too often beset by thorns; and that at times when I was supposed beguiled by the pleasures and splendours of Europe, and "treading the primrose path of dalliance," I was in fact shut up from society, battling with cares and perplexities, and almost struggling for subsistence.

In the mean time, my lengthened exile subjected me to painful doubts and surmises. Some, who really valued me, supposed that I was dazzled by the factitious splendours around me, and was leading a life of epicurean indulgence. Others, who knew me not, or chose to judge harshly, accused me of a want of affection for my native land; I met with imputations of the kind in the public papers, and I received anonymous letters, reiterating them, and basely endeavouring to persuade me that I had lost the good will of my countrymen.

4

Author's Introduction

I should have treated these imputations with little regard, but they reached me in desponding moments, when other circumstances had produced a morbid state of feelings, and they sunk deeply in my mind. The literary undertakings in which I was engaged, and on which I depended for my maintainance, required a further absence from my country, yet I found that absence attributed to motives abhorrent to my feelings, and wounding to my pride.

By degrees I was led to doubt the entire sentiment of my countrymen towards me. Perhaps I was rendered more sensitive on this head by the indulgent good will I had ever experienced from them. They had always cherished me beyond my deserts, excusing my many deficiencies, taking my humours and errors in good part, and exaggerating every merit. Their cordial kindness had in a manner become necessary to me. I was like a spoiled child, that could not bear the glance of an altered eye. I cared even less for their good opinion than their good will, and felt indignant at being elbowed into a position with respect to them, from which my soul revolted.

I was repeatedly urged by those who knew the workings of my feelings, to lay them before my countrymen, and to repel the doubts that had been cast upon my patriotism. I declined to follow their advice. I have generally been content, in all matters relating to myself, to suffer the truth to work its own way to light. If the conduct and concerns of an individual are worthy of public attention, they will sooner or later be accurately known and appreciated; and it is that ultimate opinion that alo constitutes true reputation: all transient popularity is little worth struggling for.

Beside, what was I asked to vindicate myself from—a want of affection to my native country? I should as soon think of vindicating myself from the charge of a want of love to the mother that bore me! I could not reply to such an imputation;—my heart would swell in my throat, and keep me silent.

Yet I will confess, that the arrow which had been planted in my heart, rankled and festered there. The corroding doubt that had been infused in my waking thoughts, affected my sleeping fancies. The return to my country, so long anticipated, became the constant subject of harassing dreams. I would fancy myself arrived in my native city, but the place would be so changed that I would not recognise it. I would wander through strange streets, meet with strange faces, and find every thing strange around me: or, what was worse, I would meet with those I loved, with my kindred, and the companions of my youth, but they no longer knew me, or passed me by with neglect. I cannot tell how often I have awakened from such dreary dreams, and felt a sadness at heart for hours afterwards.

At length the long anticipated moment arrived. I again saw the "blue line of my native land" rising like a cloud in that horizon where, so many years before, I had seen it fade away. I again saw the bright city of my birth rising out of its beautiful bay; its multiplied fanes and spires, and its prolonged forest of masts, proclaiming its augmented grandeur. My heart throbbed with pride and admiration as I gazed upon it—I gloried in being its son.

But how was the wanderer to be received, after such an absence? Was he to be taken, as a favoured child, to its bosom; or repulsed as a stranger, and a changeling?

My old doubts recurred as I stepped upon land. I could scarcely realize that I was indeed in my native city, among the haunts of my childhood. Might not this be another of those dreams that had so often beguiled me? There were circumstances enough to warrant such a surmise. I passed through places that ought to be familiar to me, but all were changed. Huge edifices and lofty piles had sprung up in the place of lowly tenements; the old landmarks of the city were gone; the very streets were altered.

As I passed on, I looked wistfully in every face: not one was known to me—not one! Yet I was in haunts where every visage was once familiar to me. I read the names over the doors: all were new. They were unassociated with any early recollection. The saddening conviction stole over my heart that I was a stranger in my own home! Alas! thought I, what had I to expect after such an absence!

Let not the reader be mistaken. I have no doleful picture to draw; no sorrowful demand to make upon his sympathies. It has been the lot of many a wanderer, returning after a shorter lapse of years, to find the scenes of his youth gone to ruin and decay. If I had any thing to deplore, it was the improvement of my home. It had outgrown my recollection from its very prosperity, and strangers had crowded into it from every clime, to participate in its overflowing abundance. A little while was sufficient to reconcile me to a change, the result of prosperity. My friends, too, once clustered in neighboring contiguity, in a moderate community, now scattered widely asunder, over a splendid metropolis, soon gathered together to welcome me; and never did wanderer, after such an absence, experience such a greeting. Then it was that every doubt vanished from my mind. Then it was that I felt I was indeed at home—and that it was a home of the heart! I thanked my stars that I had been born among such friends; I thanked my stars, that had conducted me back to dwell among them while I yet had the capacity to enjoy their fellowship.

It is the very reception I met with that has drawn from me these confessions. Had I experienced coldness or distrust—had I been treated as an alien from the sympathies of my countrymen, I should have buried my wounded feelings in my bosom, and remained silent. But they have welcomed me home with their old indulgence; they have shown that, notwithstanding my long absence, and the doubts and suggestions to which it had given rise, they still believe and trust in me. And now, let them feel assured, that I am heart and soul among them.

I make no boast of my patriotism; I can only say, that, as far as it goes, it is no blind attachment. I have sojourned in various countries; have been treated in them above my deserts; and the remembrance of them is grateful and pleasant to me. I have seen what is brightest and best in foreign lands, and have found, in every nation, enough to love and honour; yet, with all these recollections living in my imagination and kindling in my heart, I look round with delightful exultation upon my native land, and feel that, after all my ramblings about the world, I can be happiest at home.

And now a word or two with respect to the volume here presented to the reader.[3] Having, since my return to the United States, made a wide and varied tour, for the gratification of my curiosity, it has been supposed that I did it for the purpose of writing a book; and it has more than once been intimated in the papers, that such a work

[3] The preface to the author's revised edition begins with the sentence that follows.

Irving had originally written a very short preface to be used in both English and American editions, but "as this was my first appearance before the American public since my return, I was induced, while the work was printing, to modify the introduction so as to express my sense of the unexpected warmth with which I had been welcomed to my native place, and my general feelings on finding myself once more at home, and among my friends." (Pierre M. Irving, *The Life and Letters of Washington Irving*, III, 80.)

was actually in the press, containing scenes and sketches of the Far West.

These announcements, gratuitously made for me, before I had put pen to paper, or even contemplated any thing of the kind, have embarrassed me exceedingly. I have been like a poor actor, who finds himself announced for a part he had no thought of playing, and his appearance expected on the stage before he has committed a line to memory.

I have always had a repugnance, amounting almost to disability, to write in the face of expectation; and, in the present instance, I was expected to write about a region fruitful of wonders and adventures, and which had already been made the theme of spirit-stirring narratives from able pens; yet about which I had nothing wonderful or adventurous to offer.

Since such, however, seems to be the desire of the public, and that they take sufficient interest in my wanderings to deem them worthy of recital, I have hastened, as promptly as possible, to meet in some degree, the expectation which others have excited. For this purpose, I have, as it were, plucked a few leaves out of my memorandum book, containing a month's foray beyond the outposts of human habitation, into the wilderness of the Far West. It forms, indeed, but a small portion of an extensive tour; but it is an episode, complete as far as it goes. As such, I offer it to the public, with great diffidence. It is a simple narrative of every day occurrences; such as happen to every one who travels the prairies. I have no wonders to describe, nor any moving accidents by flood or field to narrate; and as to those who look for a marvellous or adventurous story at my hands, I can only reply in the words of the weary knife-grinder: "Story! God bless you, I have none to tell, sir."

৩১ I ৡ৵

*The Pawnee Hunting Grounds.—Travelling Companions.
—A Commissioner.—A Virtuoso.—A Seeker of Adventures.
—A Gil Blas of the Frontier.—A Young Man's Anticipations of Pleasure.*

IN THE OFTEN vaunted regions of the Far West, several hundred miles beyond the Mississippi, extends a vast tract of uninhabited country, where there is neither to be seen the log house of the white man, nor the wigwam of the Indian. It consists of great grassy plains, interspersed with forests and groves, and clumps of trees, and watered by the Arkansas, the grand Canadian, the Red River, and their tributary streams. Over these fertile and verdant wastes still roam the elk, the buffalo, and the wild horse, in all their native freedom. These, in fact, are the hunting grounds of the various tribes of the Far West. Hither repair the Osage, the Creek, the Delaware and other tribes that have linked themselves with civilization, and live within the vicinity of the white settlements. Here resort also, the Pawnees, the Comanches, and other fierce, and as yet independent tribes, the nomades of the prairies, or the inhabitants of the skirts of the Rocky Mountains. The regions I have mentioned form a debatable ground of these warring and vindictive tribes; none of them presume to erect a permanent habitation within its borders. Their hunters and "braves" repair thither in numerous bodies during the season of game, throw up their transient hunting camps, consisting of light bowers covered with bark and skins, commit sad havoc among the innumerable herds that graze the prairies, and having loaded themselves with venison and buffalo meat, warily retire from the dangerous neighborhood. These expeditions partake, always, of a warlike character; the hunters are all armed for action, offensive and defensive, and are bound to incessant vigilance. Should they, in their excursions, meet the hunters of an adverse tribe, savage conflicts take place. Their encampments, too, are always subject to be surprised by wandering war parties, and their hunters, when scattered in pursuit of game, to be captured or massacred by lurking foes. Mouldering skulls and skeletons, bleaching in some dark ravine, or near the traces of a hunting camp, occasionally mark the scene of a foregone act of blood, and let the wanderer know the dangerous nature of the region he is traversing. It is the purport of the following pages to narrate a month's excursion to these noted hunting grounds, through a tract of country which had not as yet been explored by white men.

It was early in October, 1832, that I arrived at Fort Gibson, a frontier post of the Far West, situated on the Neosho, or Grand River, near its confluence with the Arkansas. I had been travelling for a month past, with a small party from St. Louis, up the banks of the Missouri, and along the frontier line of agencies and missions, that extends from the Missouri to the Arkansas.[1] Our party was headed by one of the Commissioners appointed by the government of the United States to superintend the settlement of the Indian tribes migrating from the east to the west of the Mississippi. In the discharge of his duties, he was thus visiting the various outposts of civilization.

[1] Irving's travels from New York to Fort Gibson have been summarized in the editor's introduction. He had left St. Louis on September 15 and arrived at the fort on October 8. For his impressions of Harmony, Neosho, Hopefield, and Union missions, see *Western Journals*, 94–95, 99–100, 107–108, 110. For the history of Fort Gibson, built in 1824, see Grant Foreman, *Pioneer Days in the Early Southwest* (Cleveland, Arthur H. Clark, 1926), 57–70, and *Advancing the Frontier, 1830–1860* (Norman, University of Oklahoma Press, 1933), 35–76.

And here let me bear testimony to the merits of this worthy leader of our little band. He was a native of one of the towns of Connecticut, a man in whom a course of legal practice and political life had not been able to vitiate an innate simplicity and benevolence of heart. The greater part of his days had been passed in the bosom of his family and the society of deacons, elders, and select men, on the peaceful banks of the Connecticut; when suddenly he had been called to mount his steed, shoulder his rifle, and mingle among stark hunters, backwoodsmen, and naked savages, on the trackless wilds of the Far West.[2]

Another of my fellow-travellers was Mr. L., an Englishman by birth, but descended from a foreign stock; and who had all the buoyancy and accommodating spirit of a native of the Continent. Having rambled over many countries, he had become, to a certain degree, a citizen of the world, easily adapting himself to any change. He was a man of a thousand occupations; a botanist, a geologist, a hunter of beetles and butterflies, a musical amateur, a sketcher of no mean pretensions, in short, a complete virtuoso; added to which, he was a very indefatigable, if not always a very successful, sportsman. Never had a man more irons in the fire, and, consequently, never was man more busy nor more cheerful.[3]

[2] Henry Leavitt Ellsworth, 1791–1858. On July 23, 1832, he had been appointed one of a board of three commissioners "to visit and examine the country set apart for the emigrating Indians, west of the Mississippi." His own extremely interesting *Narrative* of this tour on the prairies, discovered and edited by Stanley T. Williams and Barbara D. Simison (*Washington Irving on the Prairie or a Narrative of a Tour of the Southwest in the Year 1832* [New York, American Book Company, 1937]), should be read in close comparison with Irving's *Western Journals* and *Tour on the Prairies*, as well as Latrobe's account to be cited below.

[3] Charles Joseph Latrobe (1801–75), nephew of the architect

My third fellow-traveller was one who had accompanied the former from Europe, and travelled with him as his Telemachus; being apt, like his prototype, to give occasional perplexity and disquiet to his Mentor. He was a young Swiss Count, scarce twenty-one years of age, full of talent and spirit, but galliard in the extreme, and prone to every kind of wild adventure.[4]

Having made this mention of my comrades, I must not pass over unnoticed, a personage of inferior rank, but of all-pervading and prevalent importance: the squire, the groom, the cook, the tent man, in a word, the factotum, and, I may add, the universal meddler and marplot of our party. This was a little swarthy, meagre, French creole, named Antoine, but familiarly dubbed Tonish; a kind of Gil Blas of the frontiers, who had passed a scrambling life, sometimes among white men, sometimes among In-

Benjamin Henry Latrobe. According to Ellsworth, Latrobe, who was traveling in the United States as tutor to Pourtalès, was "well informed, judicious, and moral in his example. . . . [He] has travelled much in Europe has read a vast deal, attended the fashionable circles" (*Narrative*, 68–69). Latrobe made a full report of his American travels with Pourtalès in *The Rambler in North America, 1832–1833* (2nd edition, 2 volumes in 1, London, 1836) and *The Rambler in Mexico* (New York, 1836). *The Rambler in North America* will hereafter be referred to as *Rambler*.

[4] Albert-Alexandre Pourtalès, Comte de Pourtalès, born in Neuchâtel, Switzerland, October 10, 1812, and died in Paris, December 18, 1861. The family estates lay in Switzerland and Bohemia; Pourtalès was later to serve as Prussian ambassador to Constantinople and to Paris. Ellsworth found him "a curious compound of character, brilliancy & fun mixed with frivolity and base sensuality—his age (19 nearing 20) is some apology, and his transatlantic indulgencies, may be added in charity—still his conduct cannot be justified, & he will later in life, look back upon his western follies (to say the least) with shame" (*Narrative*, 67). His "western follies" were his (unsuccessful) attempts to secure a temporary wife among the Osages.

dians; sometimes in the employ of traders, missionaries and
Indian agents; sometimes mingling with the Osage hunters.
We picked him up at St. Louis, near which he has a small
farm, an Indian wife, and a brood of half-blood children.
According to his own account, however, he had a wife
in every tribe; in fact, if all this little vagabond said of
himself were to be believed, he was without morals, without caste, without creed, without country, and even without language; for he spoke a jargon of mingled French,
English, and Osage. He was, withal, a notorious braggart,
and a liar of the first water. It was amusing to hear him
vapor and gasconade about his terrible exploits and hair-
breadth escapes in war and hunting. In the midst of his
volubility, he was prone to be seized by a spasmodic gasping, as if the springs of his jaws were suddenly unhinged;
but I am apt to think it was caused by some falsehood that
stuck in his throat, for I generally remarked that immediately afterward there bolted forth a lie of the first magnitude.[5]

[5] Antoine Deshetres was born in Florissant, Missouri, October 19,
1791, and married Camille Mercier (of French, *not* Indian parentage) in that town in 1812. At his death in October, 1854, he was
survived by eleven children. Irving's description of him as a mere
comic servant is amusing, but it is inaccurate and unfair to the man;
for a discussion see *Western Journals*, 49–62. Latrobe formed a
much different impression of Tonish: "Light, active, in the prime
of life, no horse could take him by surprise; no inclined plane could
throw him off his balance. He was a man of no mean qualifications.
Full of make-shifts, and unspeakably useful in the woods. . . . He
was garrulous to excess, in spite of an impediment in his speech. . . .
He was a weaver of interminable stories, all about himself and his
hunting exploits. We soon found out that he was a most determined
and audacious braggart . . . we all came to the conclusion, that, for
lying effrontery, none of us had ever seen his equal. In fact, such
was the ingenious and whimsical way in which he would bring a
host of little lies to cover a big one, that it became a matter of amusement with us to watch his manoeuvres" (*Rambler*, I, 147–48).

Our route had been a pleasant one, quartering ourselves, occasionally, at the widely separated establishments of the Indian missionaries, but in general camping out in the fine groves that border the streams, and sleeping under cover of a tent. During the latter part of our tour we had pressed forward in hopes of arriving in time at Fort Gibson to accompany the Osage hunters on their autumnal visit to the buffalo prairies.[6] Indeed the imagination of the young Count had become completely excited on the subject. The grand scenery and wild habits of the prairies had set his spirits madding, and the stories that little Tonish told him of Indian braves and Indian beauties, of hunting buffaloes and catching wild horses, had set him all agog for a dash into savage life. He was a bold and hard rider, and longed to be scouring the hunting grounds. It was amusing to hear his youthful anticipations of all that he was to see, and do, and enjoy, when mingling among the Indians and participating in their hardy adventures; and it was still more amusing to listen to the gasconadings of little Tonish, who volunteered to be his faithful squire in all his perilous undertakings; to teach him how to catch the wild horse, bring down the buffalo, and win the smiles of Indian princesses;—"And if we can only get sight of a prairie on fire!" said the young Count—"By Gar, I'll set one on fire myself!" cried the little Frenchman.

[6] They did not go out on the hunt with the Osages. The kind of experiences they might have had were excellently reported by Victor Tixier, who in 1840 did enjoy such adventures; see *Tixier's Travels on the Osage Prairies*, edited by John Francis McDermott, translated by Albert J. Salvan (Norman, University of Oklahoma Press, 1940), 186–259.

~§ II ࣸ~

Anticipations Disappointed.—New Plans.—Preparations to Join an Exploring Party.—Departure from Fort Gibson.— Fording of the Verdigris.—An Indian Cavalier.

THE ANTICIPATIONS of a young man are prone to meet with disappointment. Unfortunately for the Count's scheme of wild campaigning, before we reached the end of our journey, we heard that the Osage hunters had set forth upon their expedition to the buffalo grounds. The Count still determined, if possible, to follow on their track and overtake them, and for this purpose stopped short at the Osage Agency,[1] a few miles distant from Fort Gibson, to make inquiries and preparations. His travelling companion, Mr. L., stopped with him; while the Commissioner and myself proceeded to Fort Gibson, followed by the faithful and veracious Tonish. I hinted to him his promises to follow the Count in his campaignings, but I found the little varlet had a keen eye to self-interest. He was aware that the Commissioner, from his official duties, would remain for a long time in the country, and be likely to give him permanent employment, while the sojourn of the Count would be but transient.[2] The gasconading of the

[1] What Irving called the Osage Agency was Colonel A. P. Chouteau's Verdigris Trading Post, near the mouth of the Verdigris River, about four miles from Fort Gibson. Here were located also the Western Creek Agency, under John Campbell, and an Osage subagency. When the disappointed Pourtalès was at last convinced that they could not overtake the Osage hunters, he and Latrobe rejoined the Commissioner's party (Latrobe, *Rambler*, I, 173–74; Ellsworth, *Narrative*, 5–7, 15; *Western Journals*, 114).

[2] Latrobe wrote that at St. Louis "Mr. Irving, de Pourtalès, and myself . . . secured the services of a French creole . . . who was to

little braggart was suddenly therefore at an end. He spoke not another word to the young Count about Indians, buffaloes, and wild horses, but putting himself tacitly in the train of the Commissioner, jogged silently after us to the garrison.

On arriving at the fort, however, a new chance presented itself for a cruise on the prairies. We learnt that a company of mounted rangers,[3] or riflemen, had departed but three days previous, to make a wide exploring tour, from the Arkansas to the Red River, including a part of the Pawnee hunting grounds, where no party of white men had as yet penetrated. Here, then, was an opportunity of ranging over those dangerous and interesting regions under the safeguard of a powerful escort; for the Commissioner, in virtue of his office, could claim the service of this newly-raised corps of riflemen, and the country they were to explore was destined for the settlement of some of the migrating tribes connected with his mission.[4]

serve us in the several capacities of guide, groom, driver, valet, cook, interpreter, hunter, and jack-of-all-trades" (*Rambler*, I, 117). Government documents show, however, that Tonish was in the employ of the Commissioners West at Fort Gibson from October 10, 1832, to March 31, 1834 (23 Cong., 1 sess., *Sen. Doc. 512*, V, 292).

[3] Captain Jesse Bean's newly formed company of mounted Rangers had reported to Colonel Matthew Arbuckle, commandant of Fort Gibson, on September 14 (Arbuckle to R. Jones, AG, Fort Gibson, September 15, 1832 [A.G.O., W.R.O., National Archives]). For more about the organization of this outfit, consult *Western Journals*, 28–33, 181–86.

[4] Such authority was included in the original instructions to the commission: "a part of the mounted rangers, recently authorized to be raised by an act of Congress, will be ordered to repair to Fort Gibson, to attend you in the execution of your duties; and the commanding officer at that post will be directed to comply with any requisitions you may make upon him, in respect to the distribution of the troops . . ." (23 Cong., 1 sess., *Sen. Doc. 512*, II, 874). Ar-

Our plan was promptly formed and put into execution. A couple of Creek Indians were sent off express, by the commander of Fort Gibson, to overtake the rangers and bring them to a halt until the Commissioner and his party should be able to join them. As we should have a march of three or four days through a wild country, before we could overtake the company of rangers, an escort of fourteen mounted riflemen under the command of a lieutenant, was assigned us.[5]

We sent word to the young Count and Mr. L. at the Osage Agency, of our new plan and prospects, and invited them to accompany us. The Count, however, could not forego the delights he had promised himself in mingling with absolutely savage life. In reply, he agreed to keep with us until we should come upon the trail of the Osage hunters, when it was his fixed resolve to strike off into the wilderness in pursuit of them; and his faithful Mentor, though he grieved at the madness of the scheme, was too staunch a friend to desert him.[6] A general rendezvous of

buckle's general instructions for the employment of the rangers had been "to order them into the Indian country where you will judge their presence will be of the most importance, and keep them ranging the frontier to preserve peace and order" (Jones to Arbuckle, A.G.O., Washington, July 7, 1832). Accordingly, on October 11, Arbuckle wrote to the adjutant general that "Mr Ellsworth . . . arrived at this Post . . . determined to proceed at once to the West, I therefore sent an express to Captain Bean of the Rangers, and required him to halt with his company until Mr Ellsworth joined him, and then to govern his movements by the wishes of that Gentleman" (A.G.O., W.R.O., National Archives).

[5] First Lieutenant Joseph Pentecost. These members of Bean's company had been left behind sick, for the company on its arrival in mid-September had been suffering considerably from the measles. According to Arbuckle there were thirteen men in this escort.

[6] Ellsworth was almost certain that Latrobe was actually employed as tutor and guardian to Pourtalès (*Narrative*, 68).

our party and escort was appointed, for the following morning, at the Agency.

We now made all arrangements for prompt departure. Our baggage had hitherto been transported on a light wagon, but we were now to break our way through an untravelled country, cut up by rivers, ravines, and thickets, where a vehicle of the kind would be a complete impediment. We were to travel on horseback, in hunter's style, and with as little encumbrance as possible. Our baggage, therefore, underwent a rigid and most abstemious reduction. A pair of saddle-bags, and those by no means crammed, sufficed for each man's scanty wardrobe, and, with his great coat, were to be carried upon the steed he rode. The rest of the baggage was placed on pack-horses. Each one had a bear-skin and a couple of blankets for bedding, and there was a tent to shelter us in case of sickness or bad weather. We took care to provide ourselves with flour, coffee, and sugar, together with a small supply of salt pork for emergencies; for our main subsistence we were to depend upon the chase.[7]

Such of our horses as had not been tired out in our recent journey were taken with us as pack-horses, or supernumeraries; but as we were going on a long and rough tour, where there would be occasional hunting, and where, in case of meeting with hostile savages, the safety of the rider might depend upon the goodness of his steed, we took care to be well mounted. I procured a stout silver-gray; somewhat rough, but stanch and powerful;[8] and retained a hardy pony which I had hitherto ridden, and which, being some-

[7] But they forgot to take plates, knives, and forks (Ellsworth, *Narrative*, 12, 21).

[8] This was the horse that Tonish rode on the trip; it was later billed by Ellsworth to the Office of Indian Affairs as "one gray horse for Antoine, Interpreter & Ser^{t}," $80.

what jaded, was suffered to ramble along with the pack-horses, to be mounted only in case of emergency.

All these arrangements being made, we left Fort Gibson, on the morning of the tenth of October, and crossing the river in front of it, set off for the rendezvous at the Agency. A ride of a few miles brought us to the ford of the Verdigris, a wild rocky scene overhung with forest trees. We descended to the bank of the river and crossed in straggling file, the horses stepping cautiously from rock to rock, and in a manner feeling about for a foothold beneath the rushing and brawling stream.

Our little Frenchman, Tonish, brought up the rear with the pack-horses. He was in high glee, having experienced a kind of promotion. In our journey hitherto he had driven the wagon, which he seemed to consider a very inferior employ; now he was master of the horse.

He sat perched like a monkey behind the pack on one of the horses; he sang, he shouted, he yelped like an Indian, and ever and anon blasphemed the loitering pack-horses in his jargon of mingled French, English, and Osage, which not one of them could understand.

As we were crossing the ford we saw on the opposite shore a Creek Indian on horseback. He had paused to reconnoitre us from the brow of a rock, and formed a picturesque object, in unison with the wild scenery around him. He wore a bright blue hunting-shirt trimmed with scarlet fringe; a gayly colored handkerchief was bound round his head something like a turban, with one end hanging down beside his ear; he held a long rifle in his hand, and looked like a wild Arab on the prowl. Our loquacious and ever-meddling little Frenchman called out to him in his Babylonish jargon, but the savage having satisfied his curiosity tossed his hand in the air, turned the head of his steed, and galloping along the shore soon disappeared among the trees.

ᴥ§ III §ᴥ

*An Indian Agency.—Riflemen.—Osages, Creeks, Trappers,
Dogs, Horses, Half-breeds.—Beatte, the Huntsman.*

HAVING CROSSED the ford, we soon reached the Osage
Agency, where Col. Chouteau[1] has his offices and maga-
zines, for the despatch of Indian affairs, and the distribution of presents and supplies. It consisted of a few log
houses on the banks of the river, and presented a motley
frontier scene. Here was our escort awaiting our arrival;
some were on horseback, some on foot, some seated on
the trunks of fallen trees, some shooting at a mark. They
were a heterogeneous crew; some in frock-coats made of
green blankets; others in leathern hunting-shirts, but the
most part in marvellously ill-cut garments, much the worse
for wear, and evidently put on for rugged service.

Near by these was a group of Osages: stately fellows;
stern and simple in garb and aspect. They wore no ornaments; their dress consisted merely of blankets, leggings,
and moccasons. Their heads were bare; their hair was
cropped close, excepting a bristling ridge on the top, like
the crest of a helmet, with a long scalp lock hanging behind. They had fine Roman countenances, and broad deep
chests; and, as they generally wore their blankets wrapped
round their loins, so as to leave the bust and arms bare,

[1] Auguste Pierre Chouteau (1786–1838) of St. Louis, whom Irving had met in that city and with whom the travelers had jour-
neyed from Independence to Fort Gibson. His principal trading
establishment at this time was at the Grand Saline on the Neosho
about forty miles above Fort Gibson, where the Irving party had
stopped on October 6.

they looked like so many noble bronze figures. The Osages are the finest looking Indians I have ever seen in the West. They have not yielded sufficiently, as yet, to the influence of civilization to lay by their simple Indian garb, or to lose the habits of the hunter and the warrior; and their poverty prevents their indulging in much luxury of apparel.

In contrast to these was a gayly dressed party of Creeks. There is something, at the first glance, quite oriental in the appearance of this tribe. They dress in calico hunting-shirts of various brilliant colors, decorated with bright fringes, and belted with broad girdles, embroidered with beads: they have leggings of dressed deer skins, or of green or scarlet cloth, with embroidered knee bands and tassels: their moccasons are fancifully wrought and ornamented, and they wear gaudy handkerchiefs tastefully bound round their heads.

Besides these, there was a sprinkling of trappers, hunters, half-breeds, creoles, negroes of every hue; and all that other rabble rout of nondescript beings that keep about the frontiers, between civilized and savage life, as those equivocal birds, the bats, hover about the confines of light and darkness.

The little hamlet of the Agency was in a complete bustle; the blacksmith's shed, in particular, was a scene of preparation; a strapping negro was shoeing a horse; two half-breeds were fabricating iron spoons in which to melt lead for bullets. An old trapper, in leathern hunting frock and moccasons, had placed his rifle against a work-bench, while he superintended the operation, and gossiped about his hunting exploits; several large dogs were lounging in and out of the shop, or sleeping in the sunshine, while a little cur, with head cocked on one side, and one ear erect, was watching, with that curiosity common to little dogs, the process of shoeing the horse, as if studying the art, or waiting for his turn to be shod.

We found the Count and his companion, the Virtuoso, ready for the march. As they intended to overtake the Osages, and pass some time in hunting the buffalo and the wild horse, they had provided themselves accordingly; having, in addition to the steeds which they used for travelling, others of prime quality which were to be led when on the march, and only to be mounted for the chase.

They had, moreover, engaged the services of a young man named Antoine, a half-breed of French and Osage origin. He was to be a kind of Jack-of-all-work; to cook, to hunt, and to take care of the horses; but he had a vehement propensity to do nothing, being one of the worthless brood engendered and brought up among the missions. He was, moreover, a little spoiled by being really a handsome young fellow, an Adonis of the frontier, and still worse by fancying himself highly connected, his sister being concubine to an opulent white trader![2]

[2] Antoine Lombard, born 1810, attended the Union Mission school in 1823 and 1824. At that time he had a four-year-old sister, Ellen; it is not likely, however, that she was the "concubine" mentioned. The "opulent white trader" has not been identified. According to Latrobe (*Rambler*, I, 177–78), "indolence seemed to be the prevailing feature [of his character]. It was depicted in his heavy, sleepy, dark eye. . . . He was willing and active enough when excited, but it was no common occasion that would incite him to action. For an hour together he would stand at the camp-fire, with his cloak tightly twisted round his body, his arms motionless within, and gaze upon nothing with a fixed glance, in which there was neither life nor speculation. In form, he was an object of admiration to us all, and I suspect to himself no less. His body and limbs were most symmetrically moulded. His bust was that of an Antinous." In the narrative of this expedition Antoine Lombard is called "Antoine," and Antoine Deshetres "Tonish."

For our own parts, the Commissioner and myself were desirous, before setting out, to procure another attendant well versed in woodcraft, who might serve us as a hunter; for our little Frenchman would have his hands full when in camp, in cooking, and on the march, in taking care of the pack-horses. Such a one presented himself, or rather was recommended to us, in Pierre Beatte, a half-breed of French and Osage parentage. We were assured that he was acquainted with all parts of the country, having traversed it in all directions, both in hunting and war parties; that he would be of use both as guide and interpreter, and that he was a first-rate hunter.[3]

I confess I did not like his looks when he was first pre-

[3] In his journals Irving gave this man's name as Billet and referred to him only by surname. Ellsworth wrote it Billette, Billett, and Billet. Latrobe called him Beatte. In official documents he was listed as Pierre Bayotte, Bayatte, Beyatt, and Beatte; when he was paid off for his services on this expedition, the Office of Indian Affairs had him down as Pierre Beatte. Obviously most of these variants are American phonetic spellings of a French name.

Ellsworth called him a Quapaw Indian (*Narrative* 7, 32); Latrobe, "the son of a French Creole and a Quapaw mother" (*Rambler*, I, 178). Catlin, who talked with him in 1834, reported that Beatte bitterly resented being called a "half-breed" and introduced the artist to his father and mother (*Letters and Notes on the North American Indians* [7th edition, London, 1848], II, 93). T. B. Wheelock in his journal of the dragoon expedition of 1834 (on which Beatte served as a guide) described him as a Frenchman who had lived nearly all his life with the Indians (23 Cong., 2 sess., *Sen. Doc. No. 1*, 74). It is almost certain that he was of French, not mixed-blood parentage.

On this tour he was paid by the Indian Office $1.50 a day for thirty-four days, as guide and interpreter. Latrobe said: "we were all inclined to misjudge him at first; but before we had been a week together in the wilderness we found his value . . . when the time of parting came, we all looked upon Beatte as a friend" (*Rambler*, I, 178–79).

sented to me. He was lounging about, in an old hunting frock and metasses or leggings, of deer skin, soiled and greased, and almost japanned by constant use. He was apparently about thirty-six years of age, square and strongly built. His features were not bad, being shaped not unlike those of Napoleon, but sharpened up, with high Indian cheek bones.

Perhaps the dusky greenish hue of his complexion, aided his resemblance to an old bronze bust I had seen of the Emperor. He had, however, a sullen, saturnine expression, set off by a slouched woolen hat, and elf locks that hung about his ears.

Such was the appearance of the man, and his manners were equally unprepossessing. He was cold and laconic; made no promises or professions; stated the terms he required for the services of himself and his horse, which we thought rather high, but showed no disposition to abate them, nor any anxiety to secure our employ. He had altogether more of the red than the white man in his composition; and, as I had been taught to look upon all half-breeds with distrust, as an uncertain and faithless race, I would gladly have dispensed with the services of Pierre Beatte. We had no time, however, to look out for any one more to our taste, and had to make an arrangement with him on the spot. He then set about making his preparations for the journey, promising to join us at our evening's encampment.

One thing was yet wanting to fit me out for the Prairies —a thoroughly trustworthy steed: I was not yet mounted to my mind. The gray I had bought, though strong and serviceable, was rough. At the last moment I succeeded in getting an excellent animal; a dark bay; powerful, active, generous-spirited, and in capital condition. I mounted him with exultation, and transferred the silver-gray to Tonish, who was in such ecstasies at finding himself so completely *en Cavalier*, that I feared he might realize the ancient and well-known proverb of "a beggar on horseback."

⤙§ IV §⤙

The Departure.

THE LONG-DRAWN NOTES of a bugle at length gave the signal for departure.[1] The rangers filed off in a straggling line of march through the woods: we were soon on horseback and following on, but were detained by the irregularity of the pack-horses. They were unaccustomed to keep the line, and straggled from side to side among the thickets, in spite of all the pesting and bedeviling of Tonish; who, mounted on his gallant gray, with a long rifle on his shoulder, worried after them, bestowing a superabundance of dry blows and curses.

We soon, therefore, lost sight of our escort, but managed to keep on their track, thridding lofty forests, and entangled thickets, and passing by Indian wigwams and negro huts, until toward dusk we arrived at a frontier farm-house, owned by a settler of the name of Berryhill.[2] It was situated on a hill, below which the rangers had encamped in a circular grove, on the margin of a stream. The master of the house received us civilly, but could offer us no accommodation, for sickness prevailed in his family. He appeared himself to be in no very thriving condition, for though bulky in frame, he had a sallow, unhealthy

[1] They left Chouteau's at 2:00 P.M. on October 10 (*Western Journals*, 112).

[2] Ellsworth called him a "half-breed" (*Narrative*, 11–12); Irving in his journal implied that he was a white man (*Western Journals*, 113). Latrobe merely mentioned sleeping "in the courtyard of one of the frontier farms" (*Rambler*, I, 176).

complexion, and a whiffling double voice, shifting abruptly from a treble to a thorough-bass.

Finding his log house was a mere hospital, crowded with invalids, we ordered our tent to be pitched in the farmyard.

We had not been long encamped, when our recently engaged attendant, Beatte, the Osage half-breed, made his appearance. He came mounted on one horse and leading another, which seemed to be well packed with supplies for the expedition. Beatte was evidently an "old soldier," as to the art of taking care of himself and looking out for emergencies. Finding that he was in government employ, being engaged by the Commissioner, he had drawn rations of flour and bacon, and put them up so as to be weatherproof. In addition to the horse for the road, and for ordinary service, which was a rough, hardy animal, he had another for hunting. This was of a mixed breed like himself, being a cross of the domestic stock with the wild horse of the prairies; and a noble steed it was, of generous spirit, fine action, and admirable bottom. He had taken care to have his horses well shod at the Agency. He came prepared at all points for war or hunting; his rifle on his shoulder, his powder-horn and bullet-pouch at his side, his hunting-knife stuck in his belt, and coils of cordage at his saddle bow, which we were told were lariats, or noosed cords, used in catching the wild horse.

Thus equipped and provided, an Indian hunter on a prairie is like a cruiser on the ocean, perfectly independent of the world, and competent to self-protection and self-maintenance. He can cast himself loose from every one, shape his own course, and take care of his own fortunes. I thought Beatte seemed to feel his independence, and to consider himself superior to us all, now that we were launching into the wilderness. He maintained a half proud, half sullen look, and great taciturnity; and his first care was to unpack his horses and put them in safe quarters for the night. His whole demeanor was in perfect contrast to our vaporing, chattering, bustling little Frenchman. The latter, too, seemed jealous of this new-comer. He whispered to us that these half-breeds were a touchy, capricious people, little to be depended upon. That Beatte had evidently come prepared to take care of himself, and that, at any moment in the course of our tour, he would be liable to take some sudden disgust or affront, and abandon us at a moment's warning: having the means of shifting for himself, and being perfectly at home on the prairies.

V

Frontier Scenes.—A Lycurgus of the Border.—Lynch's
Law.—The Danger of Finding a Horse.—The Young Osage.

O<small>N</small> the following morning, (Oct. 11,) we were on
the march by half past seven o'clock, and rode through
deep rich bottoms of alluvial soil, overgrown with redundant vegetation, and trees of an enormous size. Our route
lay parallel to the west[1] bank of the Arkansas, on the
borders of which river, near the confluence of the Red
Fork, we expected to overtake the main body of rangers.
For some miles the country was sprinkled with Creek
villages and farm-houses; the inhabitants of which appeared to have adopted, with considerable facility, the
rudiments of civilization, and to have thriven in consequence. Their farms were well stocked, and their houses
had a look of comfort and abundance.

We met with numbers of them returning from one of
their grand games of ball, for which their nation is celebrated. Some were on foot, some on horseback; the latter,
occasionally, with gayly dressed females behind them.
They are a well-made race, muscular and closely knit, with
well-turned thighs and legs. They have a gypsy fondness
for brilliant colors and gay decorations, and are bright
and fanciful objects when seen at a distance on the prairies. One had a scarlet handkerchief bound round his head,
surmounted with a tuft of black feathers like a cock's tail.
Another had a white handkerchief, with red feathers;
while a third, for want of a plume, had stuck in his turban
a brilliant bunch of sumach.

[1] Probably a slip for "east." They were traveling on the north
(left) side of the Arkansas.

On the verge of the wilderness we paused to inquire our way at a log house, owned by a white settler or squatter, a tall raw-boned old fellow, with red hair, a lank lantern visage, and an inveterate habit of winking with one eye, as if everything he said was of knowing import. He was in a towering passion. One of his horses was missing; he was sure it had been stolen in the night by a straggling party of Osages encamped in a neighboring swamp; but he would have satisfaction! He would make an example of the villains. He had accordingly caught down his rifle from the wall, that invariable enforcer of right or wrong upon the frontiers, and, having saddled his steed, was about to sally forth on a foray into the swamp; while a brother squatter, with rifle in hand, stood ready to accompany him.

We endeavored to calm the old campaigner of the prairies by suggesting that his horse might have strayed into the neighboring woods; but he had the frontier propensity to charge everything to the Indians, and nothing could dissuade him from carrying fire and sword into the swamp.

After riding a few miles farther we lost the trail of the main body of rangers, and became perplexed by a variety of tracks made by the Indians and settlers. At length coming to a log house, inhabited by a white man, the very last on the frontier, we found that we had wandered from our true course.[2] Taking us back for some distance, he again brought us to the right trail; putting ourselves upon which, we took our final departure, and launched into the broad wilderness.

[2] Latrobe (*Rambler*, I, 176) mentioned that after passing through the Creek Nation they had come to "the very last white habitation at noon of the second day." Ellsworth identified this last settlement as belonging to a Mr. Hardriger, a Creek (*Narrative*, 15). According to Grant Foreman (*Advancing the Frontier*, 19–20), the man's name was Hardage.

The trail kept on like a straggling footpath, over hill and dale, through brush and brake, and tangled thicket, and open prairie. In traversing the wilds it is customary for a party either of horse or foot to follow each other in single file like the Indians; so that the leaders break the way for those who follow, and lessen their labor and fatigue. In this way, also, the number of a party is concealed, the whole leaving but one narrow well trampled track to mark their course.

We had not long regained the trail, when, on emerging from a forest, we beheld our raw-boned, hard-winking, hard-riding knight-errant of the frontier, descending the slope of a hill, followed by his companion in arms. As he drew near to us, the gauntness of his figure and ruefulness of his aspect reminded me of the description of the hero of La Mancha, and he was equally bent on affairs of doughty enterprise, being about to penetrate the thickets of the perilous swamp, within which the enemy lay ensconced.

While we were holding a parley with him on the slope of the hill, we descried an Osage on horseback issuing out of a skirt of wood about half a mile off, and leading a horse by a halter. The latter was immediately recognized by our hard-winking friend as the steed of which was in quest. As the Osage drew near, I was struck with his appearance. He was about nineteen or twenty years of age, but well grown, with the fine Roman countenance common to his tribe, and as he rode with his blanket wrapped around his loins, his naked bust would have furnished a model for a statuary. He was mounted on a beautiful piebald horse, a mottled white and brown, of the wild breed of the prairies, decorated with a broad collar, from which hung in front a tuft of horse-hair dyed of a bright scarlet.

The youth rode slowly up to us with a frank open air,

and signified by means of our interpreter Beatte, that the horse he was leading had wandered to their camp, and he was now on his way to conduct him back to his owner.

I had expected to witness an expression of gratitude on the part of our hard-favored cavalier, but to my surprise the old fellow broke out into a furious passion. He declared that the Indians had carried off his horse in the night, with the intention of bringing him home in the morning, and claiming a reward for finding him; a common practice, as he affirmed, among the Indians. He was, therefore, for tying the young Indian to a tree and giving him a sound lashing; and was quite surprised at the burst of indignation which this novel mode of requiting a service drew from us. Such, however, is too often the administration of law on the frontier, "Lynch's law," as it is technically termed, in which the plaintiff is apt to be witness, jury, judge, and executioner, and the defendant to be convicted and punished on mere presumption; and in this way, I am convinced, are occasioned many of those heart-burnings and resentments among the Indians, which lead to retaliation, and end in Indian wars. When I compared the open, noble countenance and frank demeanor of the young Osage, with the sinister visage and high-handed conduct of the frontiersman, I felt little doubt on whose back a lash would be most meritoriously bestowed.

Being thus obliged to content himself with the recovery of his horse, without the pleasure of flogging the finder into the bargain, the old Lycurgus, or rather Draco, of the frontier, set off growling on his return homeward, followed by his brother squatter.[3]

[3] Irving laid the ground for this episode in his notebooks (*Western Journals*, 113–14). Ellsworth made no mention of the frontiersman, but said that an Osage led a horse to their party about 10:00 A.M., and that some Cherokees, claiming the horse, wanted to whip him for stealing it (*Narrative*, 13). Latrobe did not report the incident.

As for the youthful Osage, we were all prepossessed in his favor; the young Count especially, with the sympathies proper to his age and incident to his character, had taken quite a fancy to him. Nothing would suit but he must have the young Osage as a companion and squire in his expedition into the wilderness. The youth was easily tempted, and, with the prospect of a safe range over the buffalo prairies and the promise of a new blanket, he turned his bridle, left the swamp and the encampment of his friends behind him, and set off to follow the Count in his wanderings in quest of the Osage hunters.

Such is the glorious independence of man in a savage state. This youth, with his rifle, his blanket, and his horse, was ready at a moment's warning to rove the world; he carried all his worldly effects with him, and in the absence of artificial wants, possessed the great secret of personal freedom. We of society are slaves, not so much to others as to ourselves; our superfluities are the chains that bind us, impeding every movement of our bodies and thwarting every impulse of our souls. Such, at least, were my speculations at the time, though I am not sure but that they took their tone from the enthusiasm of the young Count, who seemed more enchanted than ever with the wild chivalry of the prairies, and talked of putting on the Indian dress and adopting the Indian habits during the time he hoped to pass with the Osages.

VI

Trail of the Osage Hunters.—Departure of the Count and His Party.—A Deserted War Camp.—A Vagrant Dog.—The Encampment.

IN THE COURSE of the morning the trail we were pursuing was crossed by another, which struck off through the forest to the west in a direct course for the Arkansas River. Beatte, our half-breed, after considering it for a moment, pronounced it the trail of the Osage hunters; and that it must lead to the place where they had forded the river on their way to the hunting grounds.

Here then the young Count and his companion came to a halt and prepared to take leave of us. The most experienced frontiersmen in the troop remonstrated on the hazard of the undertaking. They were about to throw themselves loose in the wilderness, with no other guides, guards, or attendants, than a young ignorant half-breed, and a still younger Indian. They were embarrassed by a pack-horse and two led horses, with which they would have to make their way through matted forests, and across rivers and morasses. The Osages and Pawnees were at war, and they might fall in with some warrior party of the latter, who are ferocious foes; besides, their small number, and their valuable horses, would form a great temptation to some of the straggling bands of Osages loitering about the frontier, who might rob them of their horses in the night, and leave them destitute and on foot in the midst of the prairies.

Nothing, however, could restrain the romantic ardor of the Count for a campaign of buffalo hunting with the Osages, and he had a game spirit that seemed always stimulated by the idea of danger. His travelling companion, of discreeter age and calmer temperament, was convinced of the rashness of the enterprise; but he could not control the impetuous zeal of his youthful friend, and he was too loyal to leave him to pursue his hazardous scheme alone. To our great regret, therefore, we saw them abandon the protection of our escort, and strike off on their haphazard expedition. The old hunters of our party shook their heads, and our half-breed, Beatte, predicted all kinds of trouble to them; my only hope was, that they would soon meet with perplexities enough to cool the impetuosity of the young Count, and induce him to rejoin us. With this idea we travelled slowly, and made a considerable halt at noon. After resuming our march, we came in sight of the Arkansas. It presented a broad and rapid stream, bordered by a beach of fine sand, overgrown with willows and cotton-wood trees. Beyond the river, the eye wandered over a beautiful champaign country, of flowery plains and sloping uplands, diversified by groves and clumps of trees, and long screens of woodland; the whole wearing the aspect of complete, and even ornamental cultivation, instead of native wilderness. Not far from the river, on an open eminence, we passed through the recently deserted camping place of an Osage war party. The frames of the tents or wigwams remained, consisting of poles bent into an arch, with each end stuck into the ground: these are intertwined with twigs and branches, and covered with bark and skins. Those experienced in Indian lore, can ascertain the tribe, and whether on a hunting or a warlike expedition, by the shape and disposition of the wigwams. Beatte pointed out to us, in the present skeleton camp, the wigwam in which the chiefs had held their consultations around the council-fire; and an open area, well trampled down, on which the grand war-dance had been performed.

Pursuing our journey, as we were passing through a forest, we were met by a forlorn, half-famished dog, who came rambling along the trail, with inflamed eyes, and bewildered look. Though nearly trampled upon by the foremost rangers, he took notice of no one, but rambled heedlessly among the horses. The cry of "mad dog" was immediately raised, and one of the rangers leveled his rifle, but was stayed by the ever-ready humanity of the Commissioner. "He is blind!" said he. "It is the dog of some poor Indian, following his master by the scent. It would be a shame to kill so faithful an animal." The ranger shouldered his rifle, the dog blundered blindly through the cavalcade unhurt, and keeping his nose to the ground, continued his course along the trail, affording a rare instance of a dog surviving a bad name.

About three o'clock, we came to a recent camping-place of the company of rangers; the brands of one of their fires were still smoking; so that, according to the opinion of Beatte, they could not have passed on above a day previously. As there was a fine stream of water close by, and plenty of pea-vines for the horses, we encamped here for the night.

We had not been here long, when we heard a halloo from a distance, and beheld the young Count and his party advancing through the forest. We welcomed them to the camp with heartfelt satisfaction; for their departure upon so hazardous an expedition had caused us great uneasiness. A short experiment had convinced them of the toil and difficulty of inexperienced travellers like themselves making their way through the wilderness with such a train of horses, and such slender attendance. Fortunately, they determined to rejoin us before nightfall; one night's camping out might have cost them their horses. The Count had prevailed upon his protégé and esquire, the young Osage, to continue with him, and still calculated upon achieving great exploits with his assistance, on the buffalo prairies.

VII

News of the Rangers.—The Count and His Indian Squire.
—Halt in the Woods.—Woodland Scene.—Osage Village.
—Osage Visitors at Our Evening Camp.

IN THE MORNING EARLY, (Oct. 12,) the two Creeks who
had been sent express by the commander of Fort Gibson,
to stop the company of rangers, arrived at our encampment on their return. They had left the company encamped about fifty miles distant, in a fine place on the
Arkansas, abounding in game, where they intended to
await our arrival. This news spread animation throughout
our party, and we set out on our march at sunrise with
renewed spirit.[1]

In mounting our steeds, the young Osage attempted to
throw a blanket upon his wild horse. The fine, sensible
animal took fright, reared and recoiled. The attitudes of
the wild horse and the almost naked savage, would have
formed studies for a painter or a statuary.

I often pleased myself in the course of our march, with
noticing the appearance of the young Count and his newly-
enlisted follower, as they rode before me. Never was preux
chevalier better suited with an esquire. The Count was
well mounted, and, as I have before observed, was a bold
and graceful rider. He was fond, too, of caracoling his
horse, and dashing about in the buoyancy of youthful spirits. His dress was a gay Indian hunting frock of dressed
deer skin, setting well to the shape, dyed of a beautiful
purple, and fancifully embroidered with silks of various
colors; as if it had been the work of some Indian beauty,

[1] But not until they had some "delicious ribs of pork" for breakfast (*Western Journals*, 116).

39

to decorate a favorite chief. With this he wore leathern pantaloons and moccasons, a foraging cap, and a double-barreled gun slung by a bandoleer athwart his back: so that he was quite a picturesque figure as he managed gracefully his spirited steed.

The young Osage would ride close behind him on his wild and beautifully mottled horse, which was decorated with crimson tufts of hair. He rode with his finely-shaped head and bust naked; his blanket being girt round his waist. He carried his rifle in one hand, and managed his horse with the other, and seemed ready to dash off at a moment's warning, with his youthful leader, on any madcap foray or scamper. The Count, with the sanguine anticipations of youth, promised himself many hardy adventures and exploits in company with his youthful "brave," when we should get among the buffaloes, in the Pawnee hunting grounds.

After riding some distance, we crossed a narrow, deep stream, upon a solid bridge, the remains of an old beaver dam; the industrious community which had constructed it had all been destroyed. Above us, a streaming flight of wild geese, high in air, and making a vociferous noise, gave note of the waning year.

About half past ten o'clock we made a halt in a forest, where there was abundance of the pea-vine. Here we turned the horses loose to graze. A fire was made, water procured from an adjacent spring, and in a short time our little Frenchman, Tonish, had a pot of coffee prepared for our refreshment. While partaking of it, we were joined by an old Osage, one of a small hunting party who had recently passed this way. He was in search of his horse, which had wandered away, or been stolen. Our half-breed, Beatte, made a wry face on hearing of Osage hunters in this direction. "Until we pass those hunters," said he, "we shall see no buffaloes. They frighten away everything, like a prairie on fire."

The morning repast being over, the party amused themselves in various ways. Some shot with their rifles at a mark, others lay asleep half buried in the deep bed of foliage, with their heads resting on their saddles; others gossiped round the fire at the foot of a tree, which sent up wreaths of blue smoke among the branches. The horses banqueted luxuriously on the pea-vines, and some lay down and rolled amongst them.

We were overshadowed by lofty trees, with straight, smooth trunks, like stately columns; and as the glancing rays of the sun shone through the transparent leaves, tinted with the many-colored hues of autumn, I was reminded of the effect of sunshine among the stained windows and clustering columns of a Gothic cathedral. Indeed there is a grandeur and solemnity in our spacious forests of the West, that awaken in me the same feeling I have experienced in those vast and venerable piles, and the sound of the wind sweeping through them, supplies occasionally the deep breathings of the organ.

About noon the bugle sounded to horse, and we were again on the march, hoping to arrive at the encampment of the rangers before night; as the old Osage had assured us it was not above ten or twelve miles distant. In our course through a forest, we passed by a lonely pool, covered with the most magnificent water-lilies I had ever beheld; among which swam several wood-ducks, one of the most beautiful of water-fowl, remarkable for the gracefulness and brilliancy of its plumage.

After proceeding some distance farther, we came down upon the banks of the Arkansas, at a place where tracks of numerous horses, all entering the water, showed where a party of Osage hunters had recently crossed the river on their way to the buffalo range. After letting our horses drink in the river, we continued along its bank for a space, and then across prairies, where we saw a distant smoke, which we hoped might proceed from the encampment of the rangers. Following what we supposed to be their trail, we came to a meadow in which were a number of horses grazing: they were not, however, the horses of the troop. A little farther on, we reached a straggling Osage village, on the banks of the Arkansas.[2] Our arrival created quite a sensation. A number of old men came forward and shook hands with us all severally; while the women and children huddled together in groups, staring at us wildly, chattering and laughing among themselves. We found that all the young men of the village had departed on a hunting expedition, leaving the women and children and old men behind. Here the Commissioner made a speech from on horseback; informing his hearers of the purport of his mission, to promote a general peace among the tribes of the West, and urging them to lay aside all warlike and bloodthirsty notions, and not to make any wanton attacks upon the Pawnees. This speech being interpreted by Beatte, seemed to have a most pacifying effect upon the multitude, who promised faithfully that, as far as in them lay, the peace should not be disturbed; and indeed their age and sex gave some reason to trust that they would keep their word.[3]

Still hoping to reach the camp of the rangers before nightfall, we pushed on until twilight, when we were obliged to halt on the borders of a ravine. The rangers bivouacked under trees, at the bottom of the dell, while we pitched our tent on a rocky knoll near a running stream.

[2] Not a village in the normal sense, but a summer encampment.

[3] See Ellsworth, *Narrative*, 18–19. He estimated the population of this camp to be about five hundred.

The night came on dark and overcast, with flying clouds, and much appearance of rain. The fires of the rangers burnt brightly in the dell, and threw strong masses of light upon the robber-looking groups that were cooking, eating, and drinking around them. To add to the wildness of the scene, several Osage Indians, visitors from the village we had passed, were mingled among the men. Three of them came and seated themselves by our fire. They watched everything that was going on around them in silence, and looked like figures of monumental bronze. We gave them food and, what they most relished, coffee; for the Indians partake in the universal fondness for this beverage, which pervades the West. When they had made their supper, they stretched themselves, side by side, before the fire, and began a low nasal chant, drumming with their hands upon their breasts, by way of accompaniment. Their chant seemed to consist of regular staves, every one terminating, not in a melodious cadence, but in the abrupt interjection huh! uttered almost like a hiccup. This chant, we were told by our interpreter, Beatte, related to ourselves, our appearance, our treatment of them, and all they knew of our plans. In one part they spoke of the young Count, whose animated character and eagerness for Indian enterprise had struck their fancy, and they indulged in some waggery about him and the young Indian beauties, that produced great merriment among our half-breeds.

This mode of improvising is common throughout the savage tribes; and in this way, with a few simple inflections of the voice, they chant all their exploits in war and hunting, and occasionally indulge in a vein of comic humor and dry satire, to which the Indians appear to me much more prone than is generally imagined.

In fact, the Indians that I have had an opportunity of seeing in real life are quite different from those described

in poetry. They are by no means the stoics that they are
represented; taciturn, unbending, without a tear or a smile.
Taciturn they are, it is true, when in company with white
men, whose good-will they distrust, and whose language
they do not understand; but the white man is equally
taciturn under like circumstances. When the Indians are
among themselves, however, there cannot be greater gossips. Half their time is taken up in talking over their adventures in war and hunting, and in telling whimsical
stories. They are great mimics and buffoons, also, and
entertain themselves excessively at the expense of the
whites with whom they have associated, and who have
supposed them impressed with profound respect for their
grandeur and dignity. They are curious observers, noting
every thing in silence, but with a keen and watchful eye;
occasionally exchanging a glance or a grunt with each
other, when any thing particularly strikes them: but reserving all comments until they are alone. Then it is that
they give full scope to criticism, satire, mimicry, and
mirth.

In the course of my journey along the frontier, I have
had repeated opportunities of noticing their excitability
and boisterous merriment at their games; and have occasionally noticed a group of Osages sitting around a fire until
a late hour of the night, engaged in the most animated and
lively conversation; and at times making the woods resound with peals of laughter. As to tears, they have them
in abundance, both real and affected; at times they make a
merit of them. No one weeps more bitterly or profusely
at the death of a relative or friend: and they have stated
times when they repair to howl and lament at their graves.
I have heard doleful wailings at day break, in the neighboring Indian villages, made by some of the inhabitants, who
go out at that hour into the fields, to mourn and weep

for the dead: at such times, I am told, the tears will stream down their cheeks in torrents.

As far as I can judge, the Indian of poetical fiction is like the shepherd of pastoral romance, a mere personification of imaginary attributes.

The nasal chant of our Osage guests gradually died away; they covered their heads with their blankets and fell fast asleep, and in a little while all was silent, except the pattering of scattered rain-drops upon our tent.

In the morning our Indian visitors breakfasted with us, but the young Osage who was to act as esquire to the Count in his knight-errantry on the prairies was nowhere to be found. His wild horse, too, was missing, and, after many conjectures, we came to the conclusion that he had taken "Indian leave" of us in the night. We afterwards ascertained that he had been persuaded so to do by the Osages we had recently met with; who had represented to him the perils that would attend him in an expedition to the Pawnee hunting grounds, where he might fall into the hands of the implacable enemies of his tribe: and, what was scarcely less to be apprehended, the annoyances to which he would be subjected from the capricious and overbearing conduct of the white men; who, as I have witnessed in my own short experience, are prone to treat the poor Indians as little better than brute animals. Indeed, he had had a specimen of it himself in the narrow escape he made from the infliction of "Lynch's law," by the hard-winking worthy of the frontier, for the flagitious crime of finding a stray horse.

The disappearance of the youth was generally regretted by our party, for we had all taken a great fancy to him from his handsome, frank, and manly appearance, and the easy grace of his deportment. He was indeed a native-born gentleman. By none, however, was he so much lamented as by the young Count, who thus suddenly found himself deprived of his esquire. I regretted the departure of the Osage for his own sake, for we should have cherished him throughout the expedition, and I am convinced, from the munificent spirit of his patron, he would have returned to his tribe laden with wealth of beads and trinkets and Indian blankets.

⊸§ VIII §⊶

The Honey Camp.

THE WEATHER, which had been rainy in the night, having held up, we resumed our march at seven o'clock in the morning, in confident hope of soon arriving at the encampment of the rangers. We had not ridden above three or four miles when we came to a large tree which had recently been felled by an axe, for the wild honey contained in the hollow of its trunk, several broken flakes of which still remained. We now felt sure that the camp could not be far distant. About a couple of miles further some of the rangers set up a shout, and pointed to a number of horses grazing in a woody bottom. A few paces brought us to the brow of an elevated ridge, from whence we looked down upon the encampment.[1] It was a wild bandit, or Robin Hood, scene. In a beautiful open forest, traversed by a running stream, were booths of bark and branches, and tents of blankets, temporary shelters from the recent rain, for the rangers commonly bivouac in the open air. There were groups of rangers in every kind of uncouth garb.[2] Some were cooking at large fires made at

[1] They overtook the Rangers about 9:00 A.M. on October 13. Ellsworth at this time gives a particularly interesting description of a typical encampment (*Narrative*, 24–29). Irving made many notes for future use (*Western Journals*, 118–23).

[2] Although a uniform was to be prescribed for the Rangers, none was yet in use. Ellsworth noted that "their dress in the first place is practically (leathern dress is the uniform) the poorest clothes they have or can get . . . their appearance is that of so many poor hunters" (*Narrative*, 25). Latrobe declared that "each appeared garbed as his fancy or finances dictated" (*Rambler*, I, 180–81).

the feet of trees; some were stretching and dressing deer skins; some were shooting at a mark, and some lying about on the grass. Venison jerked, and hung on frames, was drying over the embers in one place; in another lay carcasses recently brought in by the hunters. Stacks of rifles were leaning against the trunks of the trees, and saddles, bridles, and powder-horns hanging above them, while the horses were grazing here and there among the thickets.

Our arrival at the camp was greeted with acclamation. The rangers crowded about their comrades to inquire the news from the fort; for our own part, we were received in frank simple hunter's style by Captain Bean, the commander of company; a man about forty years of age, vigorous and active. His life had been chiefly passed on the frontier, occasionally in Indian warfare, so that he was a thorough woodsman, and a first-rate hunter. He was equipped in character; in leathern hunting-shirt and leggings, and a leathern foraging cap.[3]

While we were conversing with the Captain, a veteran huntsman approached, whose whole appearance struck me. He was of the middle size, but tough and weatherproved; a head partly bald and garnished with loose iron-gray locks, and a fine black eye, beaming with youthful

[3] Jesse Bean, of Independence County, Arkansas, had fought at the Battle of New Orleans and later commanded a company of scouts under Jackson in Florida. On July 27, 1832, he had received his authorization to raise a company of Rangers (*Western Journals*, 28ff.). Ellsworth thought him "a very worthy, good natured easy sort of man—personally brave and possessing the qualities of a good woods man—He is worthy of confidence, and actuated by correct motives—But he is greatly deficient in energy and more so in discipline" (*Narrative*, 24). Though the travelers were all to comment on the lack of discipline among these troops, Latrobe spoke of their "almost unbroken good conduct" and heard or saw "nothing bordering on either insubordination or coercion" (*Rambler*, I, 192).

spirit. His dress was similar to that of the Captain, a rifle shirt and leggings of dressed deer skin, that had evidently seen service; a powder-horn was slung by his side, a hunting-knife stuck in his belt, and in his hand was an ancient and trusty rifle, doubtless as dear to him as a bosom friend. He asked permission to go hunting, which was readily granted. "That's old Ryan," said the Captain, when he had gone; "there's not a better hunter in the camp; he's sure to bring in game."[4]

In a little while our pack-horses were unloaded and turned loose to revel among the pea-vines. Our tent was pitched; our fire made; the half of a deer had been sent to us from the Captain's lodge; Beatte brought in a couple of wild turkeys; the spits were laden, and the camp-kettle crammed with meat; and to crown our luxuries, a basin filled with great flakes of delicious honey, the spoils of a plundered bee-tree, was given us by one of the rangers.[5]

Our little Frenchman, Tonish, was in an ecstacy, and tucking up his sleeves to the elbows, set to work to make a display of his culinary skill, on which he prided himself almost as much as upon his hunting, his riding, and his warlike prowess.

[4] The muster roll of Bean's company for September 26, 1832, included among the privates a John Ryan and a William Ryan who had both enlisted on August 14, at Horsehead, Arkansas (*Western Journals*, 185). Which one was "old" Ryan is not clear in the narratives of the travelers; Ellsworth referred to them as father and son (*Narrative*, 52). Obviously, the adjutant general's instructions that "the men are not to be above 40 years" were ignored in this instance. Latrobe called him "a fine old man, who, out of love for the hunter's life, had joined the expedition and the messes of those far younger and less experienced than himself" (*Rambler*, I, 192).

[5] According to Latrobe, the Rangers while waiting had cut down eighteen bee trees (*Rambler*, I, 181).

ᴇ§ IX §ᴈ

A Bee Hunt.

THE BEAUTIFUL FOREST in which we were encamped
abounded in bee-trees; that is to say, trees in the decayed
trunks of which wild bees had established their hives. It
is surprising in what countless swarms the bees have over-
spread the Far West, within but a moderate number of
years. The Indians consider them the harbinger of the
white man, as the buffalo is of the red man; and say that,
in proportion as the bee advances, the Indian and buffalo
retire. We are always accustomed to associate the hum of
the bee-hive with the farm-house and flower-garden, and
to consider those industrious little animals as connected
with the busy haunts of man, and I am told that the wild
bee is seldom to be met with at any great distance from the
frontier. They have been the heralds of civilization, stead-
fastly preceding it as it advanced from the Atlantic borders, and some of the ancient settlers of the West pretend
to give the very year when the honey-bee first crossed
the Mississippi.[1] The Indians with surprise found the
mouldering trees of their forests suddenly teeming with
ambrosial sweets, and nothing, I am told, can exceed the
greedy relish with which they banquet for the first time
upon this unbought luxury of the wilderness.

At present the honey-bee swarms in myriads, in the

[1] Richard Edwards, *Great West and her Commercial Metropolis*
(St. Louis, 1860), 590. According to a note in Edwards' book, the
first swarm of bees to appear in St. Louis settled in Mme. Chouteau's
garden in 1792.

noble groves and forests which skirt and intersect the prairies, and extend along the alluvial bottoms of the rivers. It seems to me as if these beautiful regions answer literally to the description of the land of promise, "a land flowing with milk and honey"; for the rich pasturage of the prairies is calculated to sustain herds of cattle as countless as the sands upon the sea-shore, while the flowers with which they are enamelled render them a very paradise for the nectar-seeking bee.

We had not been long in the camp when a party set out in quest of a bee-tree; and, being curious to witness the sport, I gladly accepted an invitation to accompany them. The party was headed by a veteran bee-hunter, a tall lank fellow in homespun garb that hung loosely about his limbs, and a straw hat shaped not unlike a bee-hive; a comrade, equally uncouth in garb, and without a hat, straddled along at his heels, with a long rifle on his shoulder. To these succeeded half a dozen others, some with axes and some with rifles, for no one stirs far from the camp without his fire-arms, so as to be ready either for wild deer or wild Indian.

After proceeding some distance we came to an open glade on the skirts of the forest. Here our leader halted, and then advanced quietly to a low bush, on top of which I perceived a piece of honey-comb. This I found was the bait or lure for the wild bees. Several were humming about it, and diving into its cells. When they had laden themselves with honey, they would rise into the air and dart off in a straight line, almost with the velocity of a bullet. The hunters watched attentively the course they took, and then set off in the same direction, stumbling along over twisted roots and fallen trees, with their eyes turned up to the sky. In this way they traced the honey-laden bees to their hive, in the hollow trunk of a blasted oak, where, after buzzing about for a moment, they entered a hole about sixty feet from the ground.

Two of the bee-hunters now plied their axes vigorously at the foot of the tree to level it with the ground. The mere spectators and amateurs, in the meantime, drew off to a cautious distance, to be out of the way of the falling of the tree and the vengeance of its inmates. The jarring blows of the axe seemed to have no effect in alarming or disturbing this most industrious community. They continued to ply at their usual occupations, some arriving full freighted into port, others sallying forth on new expeditions, like so many merchantmen in a money-making metropolis, little suspicious of impending bankruptcy and downfall. Even a loud crack which announced the disrupture of the trunk failed to divert their attention from the intense pursuit of gain; at length down came the tree with a tremendous crash, bursting open from end to end, and displaying all the hoarded treasures of the commonwealth.

One of the hunters immediately ran up with a wisp of lighted hay as a defense against the bees. The latter, however, made no attack and sought no revenge; they seemed stupefied by the catastrophe and unsuspicious of its cause, and remained crawling and buzzing about the ruins without offering us any molestation. Every one of the party now fell to, with spoon and hunting-knife, to scoop out the flakes of honey-comb with which the hollow trunk was stored. Some of them were of old date and a deep brown color, others were beautifully white, and the honey in their cells was almost limpid. Such of the combs as were entire were placed in camp-kettles to be conveyed to the encampment; those which had been shivered in the fall were devoured upon the spot. Every stark bee-hunter was to be seen with a rich morsel in his hand, dripping about his fingers, and disappearing as rapidly as a cream tart before the holiday appetite of a schoolboy.

Nor was it the bee-hunters alone that profited by the downfall of this industrious community; as if the bees would carry through the similitude of their habits with those of laborious and gainful man, I beheld numbers from rival hives, arriving on eager wing, to enrich themselves with the ruins of their neighbors. These busied themselves as eagerly and cheerfully as so many wreckers on an Indiaman that has been driven on shore; plunging into the cells of the broken honey-combs, banqueting greedily on the spoil, and then winging their way full freighted to their homes. As to the poor proprietors of the ruin, they seemed to have no heart to do anything, not even to taste the nectar that flowed around them; but crawled backward and forward, in vacant desolation, as I have seen a poor fellow with his hands in his breeches pockets, whistling vacantly and despondingly about the ruins of his house that had been burnt.

It is difficult to describe the bewilderment and confusion of the bees of the bankrupt hive who had been absent at the time of the catastrophe, and who arrived from time to time, with full cargoes from abroad. At first they wheeled about in the air, in the place where the fallen tree had once reared its head, astonished at finding it all a vacuum. At length, as if comprehending their disaster, they settled down in clusters on a dry branch of a neighboring tree, whence they seemed to contemplate the prostrate ruin, and to buzz forth doleful lamentations over the downfall of their republic. It was a scene on which the "melancholy Jacques" might have moralized by the hour.

We now abandoned the place, leaving much honey in the hollow of the tree. "It will be cleared off by varmint," said one of the rangers. "What vermin?" asked I. "Oh, bears, and skunks, and racoons, and 'possums. The bears is the knowingest varmint for finding out a bee-tree in the world. They'll gnaw for days together at the trunk till they make a hole big enough to get in their paws, and then they'll haul out honey, bees and all."[2]

[2] Ellsworth accompanied Irving on this bee hunt (*Narrative*, 29–31).

Amusements in the Camp.—Consultations.—Hunters' Fare and Feasting.—Evening Scenes.—Camp Melody.—The Fate of an Amateur Owl.

O<small>N RETURNING</small> to the camp, we found it a scene of the greatest hilarity. Some of the rangers were shooting at a mark, others were leaping, wrestling, and playing at prison bars.[1] They were mostly young men, on their first expedition, in high health and vigor, and buoyant with anticipations; and I can conceive nothing more likely to set the youthful blood into a flow, than a wild wood life of the kind, and the range of a magnificent wilderness, abounding with game, and fruitful of adventure. We send our youth abroad to grow luxurious and effeminate in Europe; it appears to me, that a previous tour on the prairies would be more likely to produce that manliness, simplicity, and self-dependence, most in unison with our political institutions.

While the young men were engaged in these boisterous amusements, a graver set, composed of the Captain, the Doctor,[2] and other sages and leaders of the camp, were

[1] Ellsworth noted another eternal pastime among soldiers· "a third [group was] playing cards—I have seen gamblers so intent upon their game as to play untill 12 at night by the flickering light of a few dry sticks" (*Narrative*, 31).

[2] Dr. Holt, a civilian doctor, had been employed from June 5, 1832, to attend the troops near Fort Gibson at $82 a month. On September 29, Colonel Arbuckle assigned him to Bean's Rangers. The following spring (at Fort Smith, Arkansas) he applied for a permanent appointment in the army, both Ellsworth and Irving writing letters in his behalf. Towards the close of 1833, he was still at Fort Smith, but he was then incapacitated by illness. Latrobe, too,

seated or stretched out on the grass, round a frontier map, holding a consultation about our position, and the course we were to pursue.

Our plan was to cross the Arkansas just above where the Red Fork[3] falls into it, then to keep westerly, until we should pass through a grand belt of open forest, called the Cross Timber, which ranges nearly north and south from the Arkansas to Red River; after which, we were to keep a southerly course toward the latter river.[4]

Our half-breed, Beatte, being an experienced Osage hunter, was called into the consultation. "Have you ever hunted in this direction?" said the Captain. "Yes," was the laconic reply.

"Perhaps, then, you can tell us in which direction lies the Red Fork?"

"If you keep along yonder, by the edge of the prairie, you will come to a bald hill, with a pile of stones upon it."

---

thought well of him: "a man of a thousand . . . an excellent marksman and fully accustomed to the life of hap-hazard and adventure we were prosecuting" (*Rambler*, I, 181).

3 The Cimarron.

4 Bean's official instructions from Arbuckle were to ". . . ascend the Little Red River [Red Fork or Cimarron], about sixty miles west from its junction with the Arkansas.—And then proceed due South to the Red River: which, it is presumed you will arrive on, about twenty five miles or more, West of the mouth of Faux Ouachita: from thence you will pass down between the Red River and Faux Ouachita, until you arrive near the mouth of the latter, when you will pursue a north East course until you arrive on the water of L'eau Bleu, which you will ascend to the western borders of the Cross Timbers, and from thence you will keep near the border of that Timber, until you arrive on the North Fork of the Canadian river, when you will take a course North East by East for this Post" (Arbuckle to Bean, Fort Gibson, October 5, 1832; the full text of this letter will be found in *Western Journals*, 31–33). It will presently be seen that the party turned back before crossing the Canadian River.

"I have noticed that hill as I was hunting," said the Captain.

"Well! those stones were set up by the Osages as a land mark: from that spot you may have a sight of the Red Fork."

"In that case," cried the Captain, "we shall reach the Red Fork to-morrow; then cross the Arkansas above it, into the Pawnee country, and then in two days we shall crack buffalo bones![5]"

The idea of arriving at the adventurous hunting grounds of the Pawnees, and of coming upon the traces of the buffaloes, made every eye sparkle with animation. Our further conversation was interrupted by the sharp report of a rifle at no great distance from the camp.

"That's old Ryan's rifle," exclaimed the Captain; "there's a buck down, I'll warrant!" Nor was he mistaken; for, before long, the veteran made his appearance, calling upon one of the younger rangers to return with him, and aid in bringing home the carcass.

The surrounding country, in fact, abounded with game, so that the camp was overstocked with provisions, and, as no less than twenty bee-trees had been cut down in the vicinity, every one revelled in luxury. With the wasteful

[5] Captain Bean's fondness for hunting is a recurrent theme in Ellsworth's *Narrative*. On October 19, he caused the Commissioner considerable alarm by leaving the column and getting lost: "I called the Capt to my quarters, and expressed my unwillingness to *blunder* along in this way into an enemies country & requested *him* not to leave the active command again—He said he would not—but his passion for hunting is supreme" (*Narrative*, 57–59). "If the Capt has any failings, it is his selfishness and extreeme fondness in hunting— Whenever we encamped *he* would say, 'boys none of you must hunt *this* side of the Creek *I* am going to hunt there *myself*,'" and would even tell Pourtalès to keep back until he could shoot first (*Narrative*, 101–102).

prodigality of hunters, there was a continual feasting, and scarce any one put by provision for the morrow. The cooking was conducted in hunters' style: the meat was stuck upon tapering spits of dogwood, which were thrust perpendicularly into the ground, so as to sustain the joint before the fire, where it was roasted or broiled with all its juices retained in it in a manner that would have tickled the palate of the most experienced gourmand. As much could not be said in favor of the bread. It was little more than a paste made of flour and water, and fried like fritters, in lard; though some adopted a ruder style, twisting it round the ends of sticks, and thus roasting it before the fire. In either way, I have found it extremely palatable on the prairies. No one knows the true relish of food until he has a hunter's appetite.

Before sunset, we were summoned by little Tonish to a sumptuous repast. Blankets had been spread on the ground near to the fire, upon which we took our seats. A large dish, or bowl, made from the root of a maple tree, and which we had purchased at the Indian village,[6] was placed on the ground before us, and into it were emptied the contents of one of the camp-kettles, consisting of a wild turkey hashed, together with slices of bacon and lumps of dough. Beside it was placed another bowl of similar ware, containing an ample supply of fritters. After we had discussed the hash, two wooden spits, on which the ribs of a fat buck were broiling before the fire, were removed and planted in the ground before us, with a triumphant

[6] According to Ellsworth (*Narrative*, 21–22), Pourtalès had bought three bowls, made out of knots of a tree, the largest holding four quarts and the smallest three pints. The middle sized bowl went to Ellsworth and Irving, the largest to Latrobe, Pourtalès, and Brailey, and the other to the three servants. Latrobe had contributed two clam shells apiece to their equipment, one large one for a plate and a small one for a salt cellar.

air, by little Tonish. Having no dishes, we had to proceed in hunters' style, cutting off strips and slices with our hunting-knives, and dipping them in salt and pepper. To do justice to Tonish's cookery, however, and to the keen sauce of the prairies, never have I tasted venison so delicious. With all this, our beverage was coffee, boiled in a camp-kettle, sweetened with brown sugar, and drunk out of tin cups: and such was the style of our banqueting throughout this expedition, whenever provisions were plenty, and as long as flour and coffee and sugar held out.

As the twilight thickened into night, the sentinels were marched forth to their stations around the camp; an indispensable precaution in a country infested with Indians. The encampment now presented a picturesque appearance. Camp fires were blazing and smouldering here and there among the trees, with groups of rangers round them; some seated or lying on the ground, others standing in the ruddy glare of the flames, or in shadowy relief. At some of the fires there was much boisterous mirth, where peals of laughter were mingled with loud ribald jokes and uncouth exclamations; for the troop was evidently a raw, undisciplined band, levied among the wild youngsters of the frontier, who had enlisted, some for the sake of roving adventure, and some for the purpose of getting a knowledge of the country. Many of them were the neighbors of their officers, and accustomed to regard them with the familiarity of equals and companions. None of them had any idea of the restraint and decorum of a camp, or ambition to acquire a name for exactness in a profession in which they had no intention of continuing.[7]

[7] Ellsworth observed that the Rangers "generally, were smart active men at home, good farmers & respectable citizens. They enlisted for only one year, to explore the country and expect to return to their families again when their term is out—In the meantime, they

While this boisterous merriment prevailed at some of the fires, there suddenly rose a strain of nasal melody from another, at which a choir of "vocalists" were uniting their voices in a most lugubrious psalm tune. This was led by one of the lieutenants; a tall, spare man, who we were informed had officiated as schoolmaster, singing-master, and occasionally as Methodist preacher, in one of the villages of the frontier. The chant rose solemnly and sadly in the night air, and reminded me of the description of similar canticles in the camps of the Covenanters; and, indeed, the strange medley of figures and faces and uncouth garbs, congregated together in our troop, would not have disgraced the banners of Praise-God Barebones.

In one of the intervals of this nasal psalmody, an amateur owl, as if in competition, began his dreary hooting. Immediately there was a cry throughout the camp of "Charley's owl! Charley's owl!!" It seems this "obscure bird" had visited the camp every night, and had been fired at by one of the sentinels, a half-witted lad, named Charley, who, on being called up for firing when on duty, excused

---

seemed determined, to keep up republican equality, by acknowledging no superior, and look upon grades of Commission in the army as a regulation, to effect regular soldiers, but not to extend to Rangers who ride upon their own horses" (*Narrative*, 24). Latrobe said that "to keep the file, when on march; never to leave the camp without express permission, and to obey general orders was all [the discipline] that the Captain required" (*Rambler*, I, 192). Colonel Arbuckle, a professional soldier, was certainly not displeased with these men: "The Company with very few exceptions is composed of very active young men raised on the Western Frontier and are well accustomed to the use of the Rifle.—In fact, I have not noticed a single individual of the company who I do not consider well qualified for active service" (Arbuckle to Colonel R. Jones, Adjutant General, Fort Gibson, October 6, 1832). For the roster of this company, see *Western Journals*, 181–86.

himself by saying, that he understood that owls made uncommonly good soup.[6]

One of the young rangers mimicked the cry of this bird of wisdom, who, with a simplicity little consonant with his character, came hovering within sight, and alighted on the naked branch of a tree, lit up by the blaze of our fire. The young Count immediately seized his fowling-piece, took fatal aim, and in a twinkling the poor bird of ill omen came fluttering to the ground. Charley was now called upon to make and eat his dish of owl-soup, but declined, as he had not shot the bird.

In the course of the evening, I paid a visit to the Captain's fire. It was composed of huge trunks of trees, and of sufficient magnitude to roast a buffalo whole. Here were a number of the prime hunters and leaders of the camp, some sitting, some standing, and others lying on skins or blankets before the fire, telling old frontier stories about hunting and Indian warfare.

As the night advanced, we perceived above the trees to the west, a ruddy glow flushing up the sky.

"That must be a prairie set on fire by the Osage hunters," said the Captain.

"It is at the Red Fork," said Beatte, regarding the sky. "It seems but three miles distant, yet it perhaps is twenty."

About half past eight o'clock, a beautiful pale light gradually sprang up in the east, a precursor of the rising moon. Drawing off from the Captain's lodge, I now prepared for the night's repose. I had determined to abandon the shelter of the tent, and henceforth to bivouac like the rangers. A bear-skin spread at the foot of a tree was my bed, with a pair of saddle-bags for a pillow. Wrapping myself in blankets, I stretched myself on this hunter's

[6] Charles Nelson of Batesville was the only Ranger of this given name on the company roll (*Western Journals*, 184).

couch, and soon fell into a sound and sweet sleep, from which I did not awake until the bugle sounded at daybreak.

⚜ XI ⚜

*Breaking up of the Encampment.—Picturesque March.—
Game.—Camp Scenes.—Triumph of a Young Hunter.—
Ill Success of Old Hunters.—Foul Murder of a Polecat.*

OCT. 14.) At the signal-note of the bugle, the sentinels and patrols marched in from their stations around the camp and were dismissed. The rangers were roused from their night's repose, and soon a bustling scene took place. While some cut wood, made fires, and prepared the morning's meal, others struck their foul-weather shelter of blankets, and made every preparation for departure; while others dashed about, through brush and brake, catching the horses and leading or driving them into camp.

During all this bustle the forest rang with whoops, and shouts, and peals of laughter; when all had breakfasted, packed up their effects and camp equipage, and loaded the pack-horses, the bugle sounded to saddle and mount. By eight o'clock the whole troop set off in a long straggling line, with whoop and halloo, intermingled with many an oath at the loitering pack-horses, and in a little while the forest, which for several days had been the scene of such unwonted bustle and uproar, relapsed into its primeval solitude and silence.

It was a bright sunny morning, with a pure transparent atmosphere that seemed to bathe the very heart with gladness. Our march continued parallel to the Arkansas, through a rich and varied country; sometimes we had to break our way through alluvial bottoms matted with redundant vegetation, where the gigantic trees were entangled with grape-vines, hanging like cordage from their branches; sometimes we coasted along sluggish brooks, whose feebly trickling current just served to link together a succession of glassy pools, imbedded like mirrors in the quiet bosom of the forest, reflecting its autumnal foliage, and patches of the clear blue sky. Sometimes we scrambled up broken and rocky hills, from the summits of which we had wide views stretching on one side over distant prairies diversified by groves and forests, and on the other ranging along a line of blue and shadowy hills beyond the waters of the Arkansas.

The appearance of our troop was suited to the country; stretching along in a line of upwards of half a mile in length, winding among brakes and bushes, and up and down the defiles of the hills: the men in every kind of uncouth garb, with long rifles on their shoulders, and mounted on horses of every color. The pack-horses, too, would incessantly wander from the line of march, to crop the surrounding herbage, and were banged and beaten back by Tonish and his half-breed compeers, with volleys of mongrel oaths. Every now and then the notes of the bugle, from the head of the column, would echo through the woodlands and along the hollow glens, summoning up stragglers, and announcing the line of march. The whole scene reminded me of the description given of bands of buccaneers penetrating the wilds of South America, on their plundering expeditions against the Spanish settlements.

At one time we passed through a luxuriant bottom of meadow bordered by thickets, where the tall grass was pressed down into numerous "deer beds," where those animals had couched the preceding night. Some oak trees also bore signs of having been clambered by bears, in quest of acorns, the marks of their claws being visible in the bark.

As we opened a glade of this sheltered meadow we beheld several deer bounding away in wild affright, until, having gained some distance, they would stop and gaze back, with the curiosity common to this animal, at the strange intruders into their solitudes. There was immediately a sharp report of rifles in every direction, from the young huntsmen of the troop, but they were too eager to aim surely, and the deer, unharmed, bounded away into the depths of the forest.

In the course of our march we struck the Arkansas, but found ourselves still below the Red Fork, and, as the river made deep bends, we again left its banks and continued through the woods until nearly eight o'clock, when we encamped in a beautiful basin bordered by a fine stream, and shaded by clumps of lofty oaks.[1]

The horses were now hobbled, that is to say, their fore legs were fettered with cords or leathern straps, so as to impede their movements, and prevent their wandering from the camp. They were then turned loose to graze. A number of rangers, prime hunters, started off in different directions in search of game. There was no whooping nor laughing about the camp as in the morning; all were either busy about the fires preparing the evening's repast, or reposing upon the grass. Shots were soon heard in various directions. After a time a huntsman rode into the camp with the carcass of a fine buck hanging across his horse. Shortly afterwards came in a couple of stripling hunters on foot, one of whom bore on his shoulders the body of a doe. He was evidently proud of his spoil, being probably one of his first achievements, though he and his companion were much bantered by their comrades, as young beginners who hunted in partnership.

Just as the night set in, there was a great shouting at

[1] On this day Irving's saddle girths broke, and he was thrown to the ground, much to the alarm of Ellsworth, but he suffered only shock (*Narrative*, 35).

one end of the camp, and immediately afterwards a body of young rangers came parading round the various fires, bearing one of their comrades in triumph on their shoulders. He had shot an elk for the first time in his life, and it was the first animal of the kind that had been killed on this expedition. The young huntsman, whose name was M'Lellan, was the hero of the camp for the night, and was the "father of the feast" into the bargain; for portions of his elk were seen roasting at every fire.[2]

The other hunters returned without success. The Captain had observed the tracks of a buffalo, which must have passed within a few days, and had tracked a bear for some distance until the foot-prints had disappeared. He had seen an elk, too, on the banks of the Arkansas, which walked out on a sand-bar of the river, but before he could steal round through the bushes to get a shot, it had re-entered the woods.

Our own hunter, Beatte, returned silent and sulky, from an unsuccessful hunt. As yet he had brought us in nothing, and we had depended for our supplies of venison upon the Captain's mess. Beatte was evidently mortified, for he looked down with contempt upon the rangers, as raw and inexperienced woodsmen, but little skilled in hunting; they, on the other hand, regarded Beatte with no very complacent eye, as one of an evil breed, and always spoke of him as "the Indian."

Our little Frenchman, Tonish, also, by his incessant boasting, and chattering, and gasconading, in his balderdashed dialect, had drawn upon himself the ridicule of

[2] So Irving wrote it, but there was no one of that name on the company roll. Possibly this was Private Willis McClendon of Batesville, Arkansas (*Western Journals*, 184). Ellsworth did not name the man; he said the celebration was held because it was the first elk shot on the trip, rather than the first shot by this man.

many of the wags of the troop, who amused themselves at
his expense in a kind of raillery by no means remarkable
for its delicacy; but the little varlet was so completely
fortified by vanity and self-conceit, that he was invulnerable to every joke. I must confess, however, that I felt a
little mortified at the sorry figure our retainers were making among these moss-troopers of the frontier. Even our
very equipments came in for a share of unpopularity, and
I heard many sneers at the double-barreled guns with
which we were provided against smaller game; the lads
of the West holding "shot-guns," as they call them, in
great contempt, thinking grouse, partridges, and even wild
turkeys as beneath their serious attention, and the rifle
the only fire-arm worthy of a hunter.

I was awakened before daybreak the next morning, by
the mournful howling of a wolf, who was skulking about
the purlieus of the camp, attracted by the scent of venison.
Scarcely had the first gray streak of dawn appeared, when
a youngster at one of the distant lodges, shaking off his
sleep, crowed in imitation of a cock, with a loud, clear
note and prolonged cadence, that would have done credit
to the most veteran chanticleer. He was immediately answered from another quarter, as if from a rival rooster.
The chant was echoed from lodge to lodge, and followed
by the cackling of hens, quacking of ducks, gabbling of
turkeys, and grunting of swine, until we seemed to have
been transported into the midst of a farmyard, with all its
inmates in full concern around us.

After riding a short distance this morning [October 15],
we came upon a well-worn Indian track, and following it,
scrambled to the summit of a hill, from whence we had a
wide prospect over a country diversified by rocky ridges
and waving lines of upland, and enriched by groves and
clumps of trees of varied tuft and foliage. At a distance

to the west, to our great satisfaction, we beheld the Red
Fork rolling its ruddy current to the Arkansas, and found
that we were above the point of junction.[3] We now
descended and pushed forward, with much difficulty,
through the rich alluvial bottom that borders the Arkansas. Here the trees were interwoven with grape-vines,
forming a kind of cordage, from trunk to trunk and limb
to limb; there was a thick undergrowth, also, of bush and
bramble, and such an abundance of hops, fit for gathering,
that it was difficult for our horses to force their way
through.

The soil was imprinted in many places with the tracks
of deer, and the claws of bears were to be traced on various trees. Every one was on the look-out in the hope of
starting some game, when suddenly there was a bustle and
a clamor in a distant part of the line. A bear! a bear! was
the cry. We all pressed forward to be present at the sport,
when to my infinite, though whimsical chagrin, I found it
to be our two worthies, Beatte and Tonish, perpetrating
a foul murder on a polecat, or skunk! The animal had
ensconced itself beneath the trunk of a fallen tree, whence
it kept up a vigorous defense in its peculiar style, until the
surrounding forest was in a high state of fragrance.

Gibes and jokes now broke out on all sides at the expense of the Indian hunter, and he was advised to wear
the scalp of the skunk as the only trophy of his prowess.
When they found, however, that he and Tonish were absolutely bent upon bearing off the carcass as a peculiar
dainty, there was a universal expression of disgust; and
they were regarded as little better than cannibals.

Mortified at this ignominious debut of our two hunters,

[3] "The Red Fork appeared worthy of its name, pouring down
into the main river at our feet, a turbid bright red stream, broken
by wide level sand bars and mud banks" (Latrobe, *Rambler*, I, 184).

I insisted upon their abandoning their prize and resuming their march. Beatte complied with a dogged, discontented air, and lagged behind muttering to himself. Tonish, however, with his usual buoyancy, consoled himself by vociferous eulogies on the richness and delicacy of a roasted polecat, which he swore was considered the daintiest of dishes by all experienced Indian gourmands. It was with difficulty I could silence his loquacity by repeated and peremptory commands. A Frenchman's vivacity, however, if repressed in one way, will break out in another, and Tonish now eased off his spleen by bestowing volleys of oaths and dry blows on the pack-horses. I was likely to be no gainer in the end, by my opposition to the humors of these varlets, for after a time, Beatte, who had lagged behind, rode up to the head of the line to resume his station as a guide, and I had the vexation to see the carcass of his prize, stripped of its skin, and looking like a fat sucking pig, dangling behind his saddle. I made a solemn vow, however, in secret, that our fire should not be disgraced by the cooking of that polecat.[4]

[4] Ellsworth (*Narrative*, 47, 109) and Latrobe (*Rambler*, I, 184–85) both enjoyed setting down Irving's first reaction to skunk roast—and both took care to add that Irving later came to enjoy fritters cooked in skunk grease as well as the roasted meat. In the next chapter Irving gets rid of this first skunk by throwing it in the Arkansas.

ᴥ§ XII §ᴥ

The Crossing of the Arkansas.

Wᴇ ʜᴀᴅ ɴᴏᴡ ᴀʀʀɪᴠᴇᴅ at the river, about a quarter of a mile above the junction of the Red Fork; but the banks were steep and crumbling, and the current was deep and rapid. It was impossible, therefore, to cross at this place; and we resumed our painful course through the forest, dispatching Beatte ahead, in search of a fording place. We had proceeded about a mile further, when he rejoined us, bringing intelligence of a place hard by, where the river, for a great part of its breadth, was rendered fordable by sand-bars, and the remainder might easily be swam by the horses.

Here, then, we made a halt. Some of the rangers set to work vigorously with their axes, felling trees on the edge of the river, wherewith to form rafts for the transportation of their baggage and camp equipage. Others patrolled the banks of the river farther up, in hopes of finding a better fording place; being unwilling to risk their horses in the deep channel.

It was now that our worthies, Beatte and Tonish, had an opportunity of displaying their Indian adroitness and resource. At the Osage village which we had passed a day or two before, they had procured a dry buffalo skin. This was now produced; cords were passed through a number of small eyelet holes with which it was bordered, and it was drawn up, until it formed a kind of deep trough. Sticks were then placed athwart it on the inside, to keep it in shape; our camp equipage and a part of our baggage were placed within, and the singular bark was carried down the bank and set afloat. A cord was attached to the prow, which Beatte took between his teeth, and throwing himself into the water, went ahead, towing the bark after him; while Tonish followed behind, to keep it steady and to propel it. Part of the way they had foothold, and were enabled to wade, but in the main current they were obliged to swim. The whole way, they whooped and yelled in the Indian style, until they landed safely on the opposite shore.

The Commissioner and myself were so well pleased with this Indian mode of ferriage, that we determined to trust ourselves in the buffalo hide. Our companions, the Count and Mr. L., had proceeded with the horses, along the river bank, in search of a ford which some of the rangers had discovered, about a mile and a half distant. While we were waiting for the return of our ferryman, I happened to cast my eyes upon a heap of luggage under a bush, and descried the sleek carcass of the polecat, snugly trussed up, and ready for roasting before the evening fire. I could not resist the temptation to plump it into the river, where it sunk to the bottom like a lump of lead; and thus our lodge was relieved from the bad odor which this savory viand had threatened to bring upon it.

Our men having recrossed with their cockle-shell bark, it was drawn on shore, half filled with saddles, saddle-bags, and other luggage, amounting to a hundred weight; and being again placed in the water, I was invited to take my seat. It appeared to me pretty much like the embarkation of the wise men of Gotham, who went to sea in a bowl: I stepped in, however, without hesitation, though as cautiously as possible, and sat down on the top of the luggage, the margin of the hide sinking to within a hand's breadth of the water's edge.[1] Rifles, fowling-pieces, and other articles of small bulk, were then handed in, until I protested against receiving any more freight. We then launched forth upon the stream, the bark being towed as before.

It was with a sensation half serious, half comic, that I found myself thus afloat, on the skin of a buffalo, in the midst of a wild river, surrounded by wilderness, and towed along by a half savage, whooping and yelling like a devil incarnate. To please the vanity of little Tonish, I discharged the double-barreled gun, to the right and left, when in the center of the stream.[2] The report echoed along the woody shores, and was answered by shouts from some of the rangers, to the great exultation of the little Frenchman, who took to himself the whole glory of this Indian mode of navigation.

Our voyage was accomplished happily; the Commissioner was ferried across with equal success, and all our effects were brought over in the same manner.[3] Nothing could equal the vain-glorious vaporing of little Tonish, as he strutted about the shore, and exulted in his superior skill and knowledge, to the rangers. Beatte, however, kept his proud, saturnine look, without a smile. He had a vast contempt for the ignorance of the rangers, and felt that he had been undervalued by them. His only observation was, "Dey now see de Indian good for someting, anyhow!"

[1] "He was then taken in the arms of Billet & Tonish and placed with great care in the centre of the tottering craft, and requested to sit *perfectly still*" (Ellsworth, *Narrative*, 41).

[2] According to Ellsworth, Irving was moved by a little playful vanity himself: "He soon reached the shore, and strided the sand along the beach on the opposite side as one who had just discovered and was taking possession of a new country!!—He was a short time left alone, in the Pawnee country" (*Narrative*, 41).

[3] When Ellsworth arrived at the opposite shore, he "was greeted by my friend Mr Irving, who was busily filling his little sketch book, with the interesting events of the day" (*Narrative*, 42).

The Crossing of the Arkansas

The broad, sandy shore where we had landed, was intersected by innumerable tracks of elk, deer, bears, racoons, turkeys, and water-fowl. The river scenery at this place was beautifully diversified, presenting long, shining reaches, bordered by willows and cotton-wood trees; rich bottoms, with lofty forests; among which towered enormous plane trees, and the distance was closed in by high embowered promontories. The foliage had a yellow autumnal tint, which gave to the sunny landscape the golden tone of one of the landscapes of Claude Lorraine. There was animation given to the scene, by a raft of logs and branches, on which the Captain and his prime companion, the Doctor, were ferrying their effects across the stream; and by a long line of rangers on horseback, fording the river obliquely, along a series of sand-bars, about a mile and a half distant.

XIII

The Camp of the Glen.
Camp Gossip.—Pawnees and Their Habits.—A Hunter's
Adventure.—Horses Found, and Men Lost.

BEING JOINED by the Captain and some of the rangers, we struck into the woods for about half a mile, and then entered a wild, rocky dell, bordered by two lofty ridges of limestone, which narrowed as we advanced, until they met and united; making almost an angle. Here a fine spring of water rose among the rocks, and fed a silver rill that ran the whole length of the dell, freshening the grass with which it was carpeted.

In this rocky nook we encamped, among tall trees. The rangers gradually joined us, straggling through the forest singly or in groups; some on horseback, some on foot, driving their horses before them, heavily laden with baggage, some dripping wet, having fallen into the river; for they had experienced much fatigue and trouble from the length of the ford, and the depth and rapidity of the stream. They looked not unlike banditti returning with their plunder, and the wild dell was a retreat worthy to receive them. The effect was heightened after dark, when the light of the fires was cast upon rugged looking groups of men and horses; with baggage tumbled in heaps, rifles piled against the trees, and saddles, bridles, and powder-horns hanging about their trunks.

At the encampment we were joined by the young Count and his companion, and the young half-breed, Antoine, who had all passed successfully by the ford. To my annoyance, however, I discovered that both of my horses were missing. I had supposed them in the charge of Antoine;

but he, with characteristic carelessness, had paid no heed
to them, and they had probably wandered from the line
on the opposite side of the river. It was arranged that
Beatte and Antoine should recross the river at an early
hour of the morning, in search of them.

A fat buck, and a number of wild turkeys being brought
into the camp, we managed, with the addition of a cup
of coffee, to make a comfortable supper; after which I
repaired to the Captain's lodge, which was a kind of council-fire and gossiping place for the veterans of the camp.

As we were conversing together, we observed, as on
former nights, a dusky, red glow in the west, above the
summits of the surrounding cliffs. It was again attributed
to Indian fires on the prairies; and supposed to be on the
western side of the Arkansas. If so, it was thought they
must be made by some party of Pawnees, as the Osage
hunters seldom ventured in that quarter. Our half-breeds,
however, pronounced them Osage fires; and that they were
on the opposite side of the Arkansas.

The conversation now turned upon the Pawnees, into
whose hunting grounds we were about entering. There is
always some wild untamed tribe of Indians, who form, for
a time, the terror of a frontier, and about whom all kinds
of fearful stories are told. Such, at present, was the case
with the Pawnees, who rove the regions between the Arkansas and the Red River, and the prairies of Texas. They
were represented as admirable horsemen, and always on
horseback; mounted on fleet and hardy steeds, the wild
race of the prairies. With these they roam the great plains
that extend about the Arkansas, the Red River, and through
Texas, to the Rocky Mountains; sometimes engaged in
hunting the deer and buffalo, sometimes in warlike and
predatory expeditions; for, like their counterparts, the
sons of Ishmael, their hand is against every one, and every

one's hand against them. Some of them have no fixed habitation, but dwell in tents of skin, easily packed up and transported, so that they are here to-day, and away, no one knows where, to-morrow.

One of the veteran hunters gave several anecdotes of their mode of fighting.[1] Luckless, according to his account, is the band of weary traders or hunters descried by them, in the midst of a prairie. Sometimes, they will steal upon them by stratagem, hanging with one leg over the saddle, and their bodies concealed; so that their troop at a distance has the appearance of a gang of wild horses. When they have thus gained sufficiently upon the enemy, they will suddenly raise themselves in their saddles, and come like a rushing blast, all fluttering with feathers, shaking their mantles, brandishing their weapons, and making hideous yells. In this way, they seek to strike a panic into the horses, and put them to the scamper, when they will pursue and carry them off in triumph.

The best mode of defense, according to this veteran woodsman, is to get into the covert of some wood, or thicket; or if there be none at hand, to dismount, tie the horses firmly head to head in a circle, so that they cannot break away and scatter, and resort to the shelter of a ravine, or make a hollow in the sand, where they may be screened from the shafts of the Pawnees. The latter chiefly use the bow and arrow, and are dexterous archers; circling round and round their enemy, and launching their arrows when at full speed. They are chiefly formidable on the prairies, where they have free career for their horses, and no trees to turn aside their arrows. They will rarely follow a flying enemy into the forest.

[1] Irving did not enter the anecdotes in his notebooks, but in the reversed (undated) sections several summarized impressions are written down (*Western Journals*, 137, 152, 164).

Several anecdotes, also, were given, of the secrecy and caution with which they will follow, and hang about the camp of an enemy, seeking a favorable moment for plunder or attack.

"We must now begin to keep a sharp look-out," said the Captain. "I must issue written orders, that no man shall hunt without leave, or fire off a gun, on pain of riding a wooden horse with a sharp back. I have a wild crew of young fellows, unaccustomed to frontier service. It will be difficult to teach them caution. We are now in the land of a silent, watchful, crafty people, who, when we least suspect it, may be around us, spying out all our movements, and ready to pounce upon all stragglers."

"How will you be able to keep your men from firing, if they see game while strolling around the camp?" asked one of the rangers.

"They must not take their guns with them unless they are on duty, or have permission."

"Ah, Captain!" cried the ranger, "that will never do for me. Where I go, my rifle goes. I never like to leave it behind; it's like a part of myself. There's no one will take such care of it as I, and there's nothing will take such care of me as my rifle."

"There's truth in all that," said the Captain, touched by a true hunter's sympathy. "I've had my rifle pretty nigh as long as I have had my wife, and a faithful friend it has been to me."

Here the Doctor, who is as keen a hunter as the Captain, joined in the conversation: "A neighbor of mine says, next to my rifle, I'd as leave lend you my wife."

"There's few," observed the Captain, "that take care of their rifles as they ought to be taken care of."

"Or of their wives either," replied the Doctor, with a wink.

"That's a fact," rejoined the Captain.

Word was now brought that a party of four rangers, headed by "Old Ryan," were missing. They had separated from the main body, on the opposite side of the river, when searching for a ford, and had straggled off, nobody knew whither. Many conjectures were made about them, and some apprehensions expressed for their safety.

"I should send to look after them," said the Captain, "but old Ryan is with them, and he knows how to take care of himself and of them too. If it were not for him, I would not give much for the rest; but he is as much at home in the woods or on a prairie as he would be in his own farm-yard. He's never lost, wherever he is. There's a good gang of them to stand by one another; four to watch and one to take care of the fire."

"It's a dismal thing to get lost at night in a strange and wild country," said one of the younger rangers.

"Not if you have one or two in company," said an older one. "For my part, I could feel as cheerful in this hollow as in my own home, if I had but one comrade to take turns to watch and keep the fire going. I could lie here for hours, and gaze up to that blazing star there, that seems to look down into the camp as if it were keeping guard over it."

"Aye, the stars are a kind of company to one, when you have to keep watch alone. That's a cheerful star, too, somehow; that's the evening star, the planet Venus they call it, I think."

"If that's the planet Venus," said one of the council, who, I believe, was the psalm-singing schoolmaster, "it bodes us no good; for I recollect reading in some book that the Pawnees worship that star, and sacrifice their prisoners to it.[2] So I should not feel the better for the sight of that star in this part of the country."

"Well," said the sergeant,[3] a thorough-bred woodsman, "star or no star, I have passed many a night alone in a wilder place than this, and slept sound too, I'll warrant you. Once, however, I had rather an uneasy time of it. I was belated in passing through a tract of wood, near the Tombigbee River; so I struck a light, made a fire, and turned my horse loose, while I stretched myself to sleep. By and by I heard the wolves howl. My horse came crowding near me for protection, for he was terribly frightened. I drove him off, but he returned, and drew nearer and nearer, and stood looking at me and at the fire, and dozing, and nodding, and tottering on his fore feet, for he was powerful tired. After a while, I heard a strange dismal cry. I thought at first it might be an owl. I heard it again, and then I knew it was not an owl, but must be a panther. I felt rather awkward, for I had no weapon but a double-bladed penknife. I however prepared for defense in the best way I could, and piled up small brands from the fire, to pepper him with, should he come nigh. The company of my horse now seemed a comfort to me; the poor creature laid down beside me and soon fell asleep, being so tired. I kept watch, and nodded and dozed, and started awake, and looked round, expecting to see the glaring eyes of the panther close upon me; but somehow or other, fatigue got the better of me, and I fell asleep outright. In the morning I found the tracks of a panther within sixty paces. They were as large as my two fists. He

[2] Washington Irving's nephew, John Treat Irving, Jr., visiting the Pawnee country on the Platte with Ellsworth in 1833, heard from John Dougherty, Pawnee agent, the story of such a sacrifice in the spring of that year and recorded it in his *Indian Sketches;* see *Indian Sketches, Taken During an Expedition to the Pawnee Tribes* [1833], edited by John Francis McDermott (Norman, University of Oklahoma Press, 1955), 184–88.

[3] Isaac Bean, brother of Captain Bean.

had evidently been walking backward and forward, trying to make up his mind to attack me; but luckily, he had not courage."

(Oct. 16). I awoke before daybreak.[4] The moon was shining feebly down into the glen, from among light drifting clouds; the camp fires were nearly burnt out, and the men lying about them, wrapped in blankets. With the first streak of day, our huntsman, Beatte, with Antoine, the young half-breed, set off to recross the river, in search of the stray horses, in company with several rangers who had left their rifles on the opposite shore. As the ford was deep, and they were obliged to cross in a diagonal line, against a rapid current, they had to be mounted on the tallest and strongest horses.

By eight o'clock, Beatte returned. He had found the horses, but had lost Antoine. The latter, he said, was a boy, a greenhorn, that knew nothing of the woods. He had wandered out of sight of him, and got lost. However, there were plenty more for him to fall in company with, as some of the rangers had gone astray also, and old Ryan and his party had not returned.

We waited until the morning was somewhat advanced, in hopes of being rejoined by the stragglers, but they did not make their appearance. The Captain observed that the Indians on the opposite side of the river were all well disposed to the whites; so that no serious apprehensions need be entertained for the safety of the missing. The greatest danger was, that their horses might be stolen in the night, by straggling Osages. He determined, therefore, to pro-

[4] "Mr Irving complains much of a swelling of the eye-lids and an eruption around the wrists—Doct Holt gave him a wash of the sugar of lead but salt water was his greatest relief—He thinks he is poisoned—I think it is owing to his diet which is chiefly meat, salted when eaten very highly" (Ellsworth, *Narrative,* 43–44).

ceed, leaving a rear-guard in the camp, to await their arrival.

I sat on a rock that overhung the spring at the upper part of the dell, and amused myself by watching the changing scene before me. First, the preparations for departure. Horses driven in from the purlieus of the camp; rangers riding about among rocks and bushes in quest of others that had strayed to a distance; the bustle of packing up camp equipage, and the clamor after kettles and frying-pans borrowed by one mess from another, mixed up with oaths and exclamations at restive horses, or others that had wandered away to graze after being packed: among which the voice of our little Frenchman, Tonish, was particularly to be distinguished.

The bugle sounded the signal to mount and march. The troop filed off in irregular line down the glen, and through the open forest, winding and gradually disappearing among the trees, though the clamor of voices and the notes of the bugle could be heard for some time afterward. The rear-guard remained under the trees in the lower part of the dell, some on horseback, with their rifles on their shoulders; others seated by the fire or lying on the ground, gossiping in a low, lazy tone of voice, their horses un-saddled, standing and dozing around: while one of the rangers, profiting by this interval of leisure, was shaving himself before a pocket mirror stuck against the trunk of a tree.

The clamor of voices and the notes of the bugle at length died away, and the glen relapsed into quiet and silence, broken occasionally by the low murmuring tone of the group around the fire, or the pensive whistle of some laggard among the trees; or the rustling of the yellow leaves, which the lightest breath of air brought down in wavering showers, a sign of the departing glories of the year.

XIV

Deer Shooting.—Life on the Prairies.—Beautiful Encampment.—Hunter's Luck.—Anecdotes of the Delawares and their Superstitions.

HAVING passed through the skirt of woodland bordering the river, we ascended the hills, taking a westerly course through an undulating country of "oak openings," where the eye stretched over wide tracts of hill and dale, diversified by forests, groves, and clumps of trees. As we were proceeding at a slow pace, those who were at the head of the line descried four deer grazing on a grassy slope about half a mile distant. They apparently had not perceived our approach, and continued to graze in perfect tranquillity. A young ranger obtained permission from the Captain to go in pursuit of them, and the troop halted in lengthened line, watching him in silence. Walking his horse slowly and cautiously, he made a circuit until a screen of wood intervened between him and the deer. Dismounting then, he left his horse among the trees, and creeping round a knoll, was hidden from our view. We now kept our eyes intently fixed on the deer, which continued grazing, unconscious of their danger. Presently there was the sharp report of a rifle; a fine buck made a convulsive bound and fell to the earth; his companions scampered off. Immediately our whole line of march was broken; there was a helter-skelter galloping of the youngsters of the troop, eager to get a shot at the fugitives; and one of the most conspicuous personages in the chase was our little Frenchman, Tonish, on his silver-gray; having abandoned his pack-horses at the first sight of the deer. It

was some time before our scattered forces could be re-
called by the bugle, and our march resumed.

Two or three times in the course of the day we were
interrupted by hurry-scurry scenes of the kind. The young
men of the troop were full of excitement on entering an
unexplored country abounding in game, and they were too
little accustomed to discipline or restraint to be kept in
order. No one, however, was more unmanageable than
Tonish. Having an intense conceit of his skill as a hunter,
and an irrepressible passion for display, he was continually
sallying forth, like an ill-broken hound, whenever any
game was started, and had as often to be whipped back.

At length his curiosity got a salutary check. A fat doe
came bounding along in full view of the whole line. Tonish
dismounted, levelled his rifle, and had a fair shot. The doe
kept on. He sprang upon his horse, stood up on the
saddle like a posture-master, and continued gazing after the
animal as if certain to see it fall. The doe, however, kept
on its way rejoicing; a laugh broke out along the line, the
little Frenchman slipped quietly into his saddle, began to
belabor and blaspheme the wandering pack-horses, as if
they had been to blame, and for some time we were relieved
from his vaunting and vaporing.

In one place of our march we came to the remains of
an old Indian encampment, on the banks of a fine stream,
with the moss-grown skulls of deer lying here and there
about it. As we were in the Pawnee country, it was supposed, of course, to have been a camp of those formidable
rovers; the Doctor, however, after considering the shape
and disposition of the lodges, pronounced it the camp of
some bold Delawares, who had probably made a brief dashing excursion into these dangerous hunting grounds.

Having proceeded some distance farther, we observed
a couple of figures on horseback, slowly moving parallel

to us along the edge of a naked hill about two miles distant; and apparently reconnoitering us. There was a halt, and much gazing and conjecturing. Were they Indians? If Indians, were they Pawnees? There is something exciting to the imagination and stirring to the feelings, while traversing these hostile plains, in seeing a horseman prowling along the horizon. It is like descrying a sail at sea in time of war, when it may be either a privateer or a pirate. Our conjectures were soon set at rest by reconnoitering the two horsemen through a small spyglass,[1] when they proved to be two of the men we had left at the camp, who had set out to rejoin us, and had wandered from the track.

Our march this day was animating and delightful. We were in a region of adventure; breaking our way through a country hitherto untrodden by white men, except perchance by some solitary trapper. The weather was in its perfection, temperate, genial and enlivening; a deep blue sky with a few light feathery clouds, an atmosphere of perfect transparency, an air pure and bland, and a glorious country spreading out far and wide in the golden sunshine of an autumnal day; but all silent, lifeless, without a human habitation, and apparently without a human inhabitant! It was as if a ban hung over this fair but fated region. The very Indians dared not abide here, but made it a mere scene of perilous enterprise, to hunt for a few days, and then away.

After a march of about fifteen miles west we encamped in a beautiful peninsula, made by the windings and doublings of a deep, clear, and almost motionless brook, and covered by an open grove of lofty and magnificent trees. Several hunters immediately started forth in quest of game before the noise of the camp should frighten it from the

[1] Pourtalès's opera glass (*Western Journals*, 130).

84

vicinity. Our man, Beatte, also took his rifle and went forth
alone, in a different course from the rest.

For my own part, I lay on the grass under the trees, and
built castles in the clouds, and indulged in the very luxury
of rural repose. Indeed I can scarcely conceive a kind
of life more calculated to put both mind and body in a
healthful tone. A morning's ride of several hours diversified
by hunting incidents; an encampment in the afternoon under some noble grove on the borders of a stream; an evening banquet of venison, fresh killed, roasted, or broiled,
on the coals; turkeys just from the thickets and wild honey
from the trees; and all relished with an appetite unknown
to the gourmets of the cities. And at night—such sweet
sleeping in the open air, or waking and gazing at the moon
and stars, shining between the trees!

On the present occasion, however, we had not much
reason to boast of our larder. But one deer had been killed
during the day, and none of that had reached our lodge.
We were fain, therefore, to stay our keen appetites by some
scraps of turkey brought from the last encampment, eked
out with a slice or two of salt pork. This scarcity, however, did not continue long. Before dark a young hunter
returned well laden with spoil. He had shot a deer, cut it
up in an artist-like style, and, putting the meat in a kind
of sack made of the hide, had slung it across his shoulder
and trudged with it to camp.

Not long after, Beatte made his appearance with a fat
doe across his horse. It was the first game he had brought
in, and I was glad to see him with a trophy that might
efface the memory of the polecat. He laid the carcass down
by our fire without saying a word, and then turned to unsaddle his horse; nor could any questions from us about
his hunting draw from him more than laconic replies. If
Beatte, however, observed this Indian taciturnity about

what he had done, Tonish made up for it by boasting of what he meant to do. Now that we were in a good hunting country he meant to take the field, and, if we would take his word for it, our lodge would henceforth be overwhelmed with game. Luckily his talking did not prevent his working, the doe was skilfully dissected, several fat ribs roasted before the fire, the coffee kettle replenished, and in a little while we were enabled to indemnify ourselves luxuriously for our late meagre repast.

The Captain did not return until late, and he returned empty handed. He had been in pursuit of his usual game, the deer, when he came upon the tracks of a gang of about sixty elk. Having never killed an animal of the kind, and the elk being at this moment an object of ambition among all the veteran hunters of the camp, he abandoned his pursuit of the deer, and followed the newly discovered track. After some time he came in sight of the elk, and had several fair chances of a shot, but was anxious to bring down a large buck, which kept in the advance. Finding at length there was danger of the whole gang escaping him, he fired at a doe. The shot took effect, but the animal had sufficient strength to keep on for a time with its companions. From the tracks of blood he felt confident it was mortally wounded, but evening came on, he could not keep the trail, and had to give up the search until morning.

Old Ryan and his little band had not yet rejoined us, neither had our young half-breed Antoine made his appearance. It was determined, therefore, to remain at our encampment for the following day, to give time for all stragglers to arrive.

The conversation this evening, among the old huntsmen, turned upon the Delaware tribe, one of whose encampments we had passed in the course of the day; and anecdotes were given of their prowess in war and dexterity in hunting. They used to be deadly foes of the Osages, who stood in great awe of their desperate valor, though they were apt to attribute it to a whimsical cause. "Look at the Delawares," would they say, "dey got short leg—no can run—must stand and fight a great heap." In fact the Delawares are rather short legged, while the Osages are remarkable for length of limb.

The expeditions of the Delawares, whether of war or hunting, are wide and fearless; a small band of them will penetrate far into these dangerous and hostile wilds, and will push their encampments even to the Rocky Mountains. This daring temper may be in some measure encouraged by one of the superstitions of their creed. They believe that a guardian spirit, in the form of a great eagle, watches over them, hovering in the sky, far out of sight. Sometimes, when well pleased with them, he wheels down into the lower regions, and may be seen circling with widespread wings against the white clouds; at such time the seasons are propitious, the corn grows finely, and they have great success in hunting. Sometimes, however, he is angry, and then he vents his rage in the thunder, which is his voice, and the lightning, which is the flashing of his eye, and strikes dead the object of his displeasure.

The Delawares make sacrifices to this spirit, who occasionally lets drop a feather from his wing in token of satisfaction. These feathers render the wearer invisible, and invulnerable. Indeed, the Indians generally consider the feathers of the eagle possessed of occult and sovereign virtues.

At one time a party of the Delawares, in the course of a bold excursion into the Pawnee hunting grounds, were surrounded on one of the great plains, and nearly destroyed. The remnant took refuge on the summit of one of those isolated and conical hills which rise almost like artificial mounds, from the midst of the prairies. Here the chief warrior, driven almost to despair, sacrificed his horse to the tutelar spirit. Suddenly an enormous eagle, rushing down from the sky, bore off the victim in his talons, and mounting into the air, dropped a quill feather from his wing. The chief caught it up with joy, bound it to his forehead, and, leading his followers down the hill, cut his way through the enemy with great slaughter, and without any one of his party receiving a wound.[2]

[2] These anecdotes about the Delaware may have originally been set down in the notebook (now missing) for October 18–30; they are not mentioned in the entries for October 16 or 17. There are, however, several paragraphs about the Delaware in the reversed portions of some of the notebooks; see *Western Journals*, 87, 164.

XV

The Search for the Elk.—Pawnee Stories.

WITH THE MORNING DAWN [October 17], the prime hunters of the camp were all on the alert, and set off in different directions, to beat up the country for game. The Captain's brother, Sergeant Bean, was among the first, and returned before breakfast with success, having killed a fat doe, almost within the purlieus of the camp.

When breakfast was over, the Captain mounted his horse, to go in quest of the elk which he had wounded on the preceding evening; and which, he was persuaded, had received its death wound. I determined to join him in the search, and we accordingly sallied forth together, accompanied also by his brother, the sergeant, and a lieutenant. Two rangers followed on foot, to bring home the carcass of the doe which the sergeant had killed. We had not ridden far, when we came to where it lay, on the side of a hill, in the midst of a beautiful woodland scene. The two rangers immediately fell to work, with true hunters' skill, to dismember it, and prepare it for transportation to the camp, while we continued on our course. We passed along sloping hillsides, among skirts of thicket and scattered forest trees, until we came to a place where the long herbage was pressed down with numerous elk beds. Here the Captain had first roused the gang of elks, and, after looking about diligently for a little while, he pointed out their "trail," the foot-prints of which were as large as those of horned cattle. He now put himself upon the track, and went quietly forward, the rest of us following him in Indian file. At length he halted at the place where the elk had been when shot at. Spots of blood on the surrounding herbage showed that the shot had been effective. The wounded animal had evidently kept for some distance with the rest of the herd, as could be seen by sprinkling of blood here and there, on the shrubs and weeds bordering the trail. These at length suddenly disappeared. "Somewhere hereabout," said the Captain, "the elk must have turned off from the gang. Whenever they feel themselves mortally wounded, they will turn aside, and seek some out-of-the-way place to die alone."

There was something in this picture of the last moments of a wounded deer, to touch the sympathies of one not hardened to the gentle disports of the chase; such sympathies, however, are but transient. Man is naturally an animal of prey; and, however changed by civilization, will readily relapse into his instinct for destruction. I found my ravenous and sanguinary propensities daily growing stronger upon the prairies.

After looking about for a little while, the Captain succeeded in finding the separate trail of the wounded elk, which turned off almost at right angles from that of the herd, and entered an open forest of scattered trees. The traces of blood became more faint and rare, and occurred at greater distances: at length they ceased altogether, and the ground was so hard, and the herbage so much parched and withered, that the foot-prints of the animal could no longer be perceived.

"The elk must lie somewhere in this neighborhood," said the Captain, "as you may know by those turkey-buzzards wheeling about in the air: for they always hover in that way above some carcass. However, the dead elk cannot get away, so let us follow the trail of the living

ones: they may have halted at no great distance, and we
may find them grazing, and get another crack at them."

We accordingly returned, and resumed the trail of the
elks, which led us a straggling course over hill and dale,
covered with scattered oaks. Every now and then we would
catch a glimpse of a deer bounding away across some glade
of the forest, but the Captain was not to be diverted from
his elk hunt by such inferior game. A large flock of wild
turkeys, too, were roused by the trampling of our horses;
some scampered off as fast as their long legs could carry
them; others fluttered up into the trees, where they remained with outstretched necks, gazing at us. The Captain
would not allow a rifle to be discharged at them, lest it
should alarm the elk, which he hoped to find in the vicinity. At length we came to where the forest ended in a steep
bank, and the Red Fork wound its way below us, between broad sandy shores. The trail descended the bank,
and we could trace it, with our eyes, across the level sands,
until it terminated in the river, which, it was evident, the
gang had forded on the preceding evening.

"It is needless to follow on any further," said the Captain. "The elk must have been much frightened, and, after
crossing the river, may have kept on for twenty miles
without stopping."

Our little party now divided, the lieutenant and sergeant
making a circuit in quest of game, and the Captain and myself taking the direction of the camp. On our way, we
came to a buffalo track, more than a year old. It was not
wider than an ordinary footpath, and worn deep into the
soil; for these animals follow each other in single file.
Shortly afterward, we met two rangers on foot, hunting.
They had wounded an elk, but he had escaped; and in pursuing him, had found the one shot by the Captain on the

preceding evening. They turned back, and conducted us to it. It was a noble animal, as large as a yearling heifer, and lay in an open part of the forest, about a mile and a half distant from the place where it had been shot. The turkey-buzzards, which we had previously noticed, were wheeling in the air above it. The observation of the Captain seemed verified. The poor animal, as life was ebbing away, had apparently abandoned its unhurt companions, and turned aside to die alone.

The Captain and the two rangers forthwith fell to work, with their hunting-knives, to flay and cut up the carcass. It was already tainted on the inside, but ample collops were cut from the ribs and haunches, and laid in a heap on the outstretched hide. Holes were then cut along the border of the hide, raw thongs were passed through them, and the whole drawn up like a sack, which was swung behind the Captain's saddle. All this while, the turkey-buzzards were soaring overhead, waiting for our departure, to swoop down and banquet on the carcass.

The wreck of the poor elk being thus dismantled, the Captain and myself mounted our horses, and jogged back to the camp, while the two rangers resumed their hunting.

On reaching the camp, I found there our young half-breed, Antoine. After separating from Beatte, in the search after the stray horses on the other side of the Arkansas, he had fallen upon a wrong track, which he followed for several miles, when he overtook old Ryan and his party, and found he had been following their traces.

They all forded the Arkansas about eight miles above our crossing place, and found their way to our late encampment in the glen, where the rear-guard we had left behind was waiting for them. Antoine, being well mounted, and somewhat impatient to rejoin us, had pushed on alone, following our trail, to our present encampment, and bringing the carcass of a young bear which he had killed.

Our camp, during the residue of the day, presented a mingled picture of bustle and repose. Some of the men were busy round the fires, jerking and roasting venison and bear's meat, to be packed up as a future supply. Some were stretching and dressing the skins of the animals they had killed; others were washing their clothes in the brook, and hanging them on the bushes to dry;[1] while many were lying on the grass, and lazily gossiping in the shade. Every now and then a hunter would return, on horseback or on foot, laden with game, or empty handed. Those who brought home any spoil, deposited it at the Captain's fire, and then filed off to their respective messes, to relate their day's exploits to their companions. The game killed at this camp consisted of six deer, one elk, two bears, and six or eight turkeys.

During the last two or three days, since their wild Indian achievement in navigating the river, our retainers had risen in consequence among the rangers; and now I found Tonish making himself a complete oracle among some of the raw and inexperienced recruits, who had never been in the wilderness. He had continually a knot hanging about him, and listening to his extravagant tales about the Pawnees, with whom he pretended to have had fearful encounters. His representations, in fact, were calculated to inspire his hearers with an awful idea of the foe into whose lands they were intruding. According to his accounts, the rifle of the white man was no match for the bow and arrow of the Pawnee. When the rifle was once discharged, it took time and trouble to load it again, and in the meantime the enemy could keep on launching his shafts as fast as he could draw his bow. Then the Pawnee, according to

[1] "Mr Irving & myself went to the Creek and washed our linnen & wollens—it was a *new employment to both*" (*Narrative*, 46).

Tonish, could shoot, with unerring aim, three hundred yards, and send his arrow clean through and through a buffalo; nay, he had known a Pawnee shaft to pass through one buffalo and wound another. And then the way the Pawnees sheltered themselves from the shots of their enemy: they would hang with one leg over the saddle, crouching their bodies along the opposite side of the horse, and would shoot their arrows from under his neck, while at full speed!

If Tonish was to be believed, there was peril at every step in these debatable grounds of the Indian tribes. Pawnees lurked unseen among the thickets and ravines. They had their scouts and sentinels on the summit of the mounds which command a view over the prairies, where they lay crouched in the tall grass; only now and then raising their heads to watch the movements of any war or hunting party that might be passing in lengthened line below. At night, they would lurk round an encampment; crawling through the grass, and imitating the movements of a wolf, so as to deceive the sentinel on the outpost, until, having arrived sufficiently near, they would speed an arrow through his heart, and retreat undiscovered.[2] In telling his stories, Tonish would appeal from time to time to Beatte, for the truth of what he said; the only reply would be a nod or shrug of the shoulders; the latter being divided in mind between a distaste for the gasconading spirit of his comrade, and a sovereign contempt for the inexperience of the young rangers in all that he considered true knowledge.

[2] For an account of Pawnee fighting tactics, see Chapter XIII.

ᴥᔐ XVI ᔑᴥ

A Sick Camp.—The March.—The Disabled Horse.—Old Ryan and the Stragglers.—Symptoms of Change of Weather, and Change of Humors.

Oᴄᴛ. 18.[1] We prepared to march at the usual hour, but word was brought to the Captain that three of the rangers, who had been attacked with the measles, were unable to proceed, and that another one was missing. The last was an old frontiersman, by the name of Sawyer, who had gained years without experience; and having sallied forth to hunt, on the preceding day, had probably lost his way on the prairies.[2] A guard of ten men was, therefore, left to take care of the sick, and wait for the straggler. If the former recovered sufficiently in the course of two or three days, they were to rejoin the main body, otherwise to be escorted back to the garrison.[3]

[1] The original notebook for October 18–30 has not been found. The reader can make a close comparison of the next seventeen chapters with Ellsworth's *Narrative*, 49–128.

[2] William Sawyers of Spadra, Arkansas. "A comical old fellow, the butt of the troop. . . . He was one of those strange mixtures of simplicity and shrewdness you sometimes meet with. . . . Sawyer generally asked for a furlough three times a day when in camp, and was celebrated for losing himself, and spending the night nobody knew where. He was used as a 'cat's-paw' by the men, whenever they wished to pry into the plans and designs of the officers" (*Rambler*, I, 195–96). Ellsworth reported his return on this occasion (*Narrative*, 50).

[3] Some of these men did return to Fort Gibson. Ellsworth sent a letter to his wife by them (*Narrative*, 49–50); and it was from this place that Irving dispatched the letter to his sister, Mrs. Paris, dated "Greenpoint, near the Red Fork of the Arkansas, October 18, 1832" (Pierre M. Irving, *The Life and Letters of Washington Irving*, III, 23–24).

Taking our leave of the sick camp, we shaped our course westward, along the heads of small streams, all wandering, in deep ravines, towards the Red Fork. The land was high and undulating, or "rolling," as it is termed in the West; with a poor hungry soil mingled with the sandstone, which is unusual in this part of the country, and checkered with harsh forests of post-oak and black-jack.

In the course of the morning, I received a lesson on the importance of being chary of one's steed on the prairies. The one I rode surpassed in action most horses of the troop, and was of great mettle and a generous spirit. In crossing the deep ravines, he would scramble up the steep banks like a cat, and was always for leaping the narrow runs of water. I was not aware of the imprudence of indulging him in such exertions, until, in leaping him across a small brook, I felt him immediately falter beneath me. He limped forward a short distance, but soon fell stark lame, having sprained his shoulder. What was to be done? He could not keep up with the troop, and was too valuable to be abandoned on the prairie.[4] The only alternative was to send him back to join the invalids in the sick camp, and to share their fortunes. Nobody, however, seemed disposed to lead him back, although I offered a liberal reward. Either the stories of Tonish about the Pawnees had spread an apprehension of lurking foes, and imminent perils on the prairies; or there was a fear of missing the trail and getting lost. At length two young men stepped forward and agreed to go in company, so that, should they be benighted on the prairies, there might be one to watch while the other slept.

The horse was accordingly consigned to their care, and I looked after him with a rueful eye, as he limped off, for

[4] This horse he had bought at Chouteau's Verdigris Trading Post for $125.

it seemed as if, with him, all strength and buoyancy had departed from me.

I looked round for a steed to supply his place, and fixed my eyes upon the gallant gray which I had transferred at the Agency to Tonish. The moment, however, that I hinted about his dismounting and taking up with the supernumerary pony, the little varlet broke out into vociferous remonstrances and lamentations, gasping and almost strangling, in his eagerness to give vent to them. I saw that to unhorse him would be to prostrate his spirit and cut his vanity to the quick. I had not the heart to inflict such a wound, or to bring down the poor devil from his transient vain-glory; so I left him in possession of his gallant gray; and contented myself with shifting my saddle to the jaded pony.

I was now sensible of the complete reverse to which a horseman is exposed on the prairies. I felt how completely the spirit of the rider depended upon his steed. I had hitherto been able to make excursions at will from the line, and to gallop in pursuit of any object of interest or curiosity. I was now reduced to the tone of the jaded animal I bestrode, and doomed to plod on patiently and slowly after my file leader. Above all, I was made conscious how unwise it is, on expeditions of the kind, where a man's life may depend upon the strength, and speed, and freshness of his horse, to task the generous animal by any unnecessary exertion of his powers.

I have observed that the wary and experienced huntsman and traveller of the prairies is always sparing of his horse, when on a journey; never, except in emergency, putting him off of a walk. The regular journeyings of frontiersmen and Indians, when on a long march seldom exceed above fifteen miles a day, and are generally about ten or twelve, and they never indulge in capricious galloping. Many of those, however, with whom I was travelling, were young and inexperienced, and full of excitement at finding themselves in a country abounding in game. It was impossible to retain them in the sobriety of a march, or to keep them to the line. As we broke our way through the coverts and ravines, and the deer started up and scampered off to the right and left, the rifle balls would whiz after them, and our young hunters dash off in pursuit. At one time they made a grand burst after what they supposed to be a gang of bears, but soon pulled up on discovering them to be black wolves, prowling in company.

After a march of about twelve miles we encamped, a little after mid-day, on the borders of a brook which loitered through a deep ravine.[5] In the course of the afternoon old Ryan, the Nestor of the camp, made his appearance, followed by his little band of stragglers. He was greeted with joyful acclamations, which showed the estimation in which he was held by his brother woodmen. The little band came laden with venison; a fine haunch of which the veteran hunter laid, as a present, by the Captain's fire.

Our men, Beatte and Tonish, both sallied forth, early in the afternoon, to hunt. Towards evening the former returned, with a fine buck across his horse. He laid it down, as usual, in silence, and proceeded to unsaddle and turn his horse loose. Tonish came back without any game, but with much more glory; having made several capital shots, though unluckily the wounded deer had all escaped him.

There was an abundant supply of meat in the camp; for besides other game, three elk had been killed. The wary and veteran woodmen were all busy jerking meat, against

[5] The day was very warm. Irving took off his pantaloons and rode in his deerskin leggings and a pair of drawers Ellsworth had lent him (*Narrative*, 51–52).

a time of scarcity; the less experienced revelled in present abundance, leaving the morrow to provide for itself.

On the following morning, (Oct. 19,) I succeeded in changing my pony and a reasonable sum of money for a strong and active horse. It was a great satisfaction to find myself once more tolerably well mounted. I perceived, however, that there would be little difficulty in making a selection from among the troop, for the rangers had all that propensity for "swapping," or, as they term it, "trading," which pervades the West. In the course of our expedition, there was scarce a horse, rifle, powder-horn, or blanket, that did not change owners several times; and one keen "trader" boasted of having by dint of frequent bargains changed a bad horse into a good one, and put a hundred dollars in his pocket.[6]

The morning was lowering and sultry, with low muttering of distant thunder. The change of weather had its effect upon the spirits of the troop. The camp was unusually sober and quiet; there was none of the accustomed farmyard melody of crowing and cackling at daybreak; none of the bursts of merriment, the loud jokes and banterings, that had commonly prevailed during the bustle of equipment. Now and then might be heard a short strain of a song, a faint laugh, or a solitary whistle; but, in general, every one went silently and doggedly about the duties of the camp, or the preparations for departure.

When the time arrived to saddle and mount, five horses were reported as missing; although all the woods and thickets had been beaten up for some distance round the camp. Several rangers were dispatched to "skir" the country

[6] Latrobe wrote at length on this passion for "swopping"; according to him, one man traded his horse so often that he returned to Fort Gibson with his own original horse and sixty dollars in cash (*Rambler*, I, 194–95).

round in quest of them. In the meantime, the thunder continued to growl, and we had a passing shower. The horses, like their riders, were affected by the change of weather. They stood here and there about the camp, some saddled and bridled, others loose, but all spiritless and dozing, with stooping head, one hind leg partly drawn up so as to rest on the point of the hoof, and the whole hide reeking with the rain, and sending up wreaths of vapor. The men, too, waited in listless groups the return of their comrades who had gone in quest of the horses; now and then turning up an anxious eye to the drifting clouds, which boded an approaching storm. Gloomy weather inspires gloomy thoughts. Some expressed fears that we were dogged by some party of Indians, who had stolen the horses in the night. The most prevalent apprehension, however, was that they had returned on their traces to our last encampment, or had started off on a direct line for Fort Gibson. In this respect, the instinct of horses is said to resemble that of the pigeon. They will strike for home by a direct course, passing through tracts of wilderness which they have never before traversed.

After delaying until the morning was somewhat advanced, a lieutenant with a guard was appointed to await the return of the rangers, and we set off on our day's journey, considerably reduced in numbers; much, as I thought, to the discomposure of some of the troop, who intimated that we might prove too weak-handed, in case of an encounter with the Pawnees.

⋐§ XVII §⋑

*Thunder-Storm on the Prairies. The Storm Encampment.
—Night Scene.—Indian Stories.—A Frightened Horse.*

OUR MARCH for a part of the day lay a little to the south of west, through straggling forests of the kind of low scrubbed trees already mentioned, called "post-oaks" and "black-jacks." The soil of these "oak barrens" is loose and unsound; being little better at times than a mere quicksand, in which, in rainy weather, the horse's hoof slips from side to side, and now and then sinks in a rotten, spongy turf, to the fetlock. Such was the case at present in consequence of successive thunder-showers, through which we draggled along in dogged silence. Several deer were roused by our approach, and scudded across the forest glades; but no one, as formerly, broke the line of march to pursue them. At one time, we passed the bones and horns of a buffalo, and at another time a buffalo track, not above three days old. These signs of the vicinity of this grand game of the prairies, had a reviving effect on the spirits of our huntsmen; but it was of transient duration.

In crossing a prairie of moderate extent, rendered little better than a slippery bog by the recent showers, we were overtaken by a violent thunder-gust. The rain came rattling upon us in torrents, and spattered up like steam along the ground; the whole landscape was suddenly wrapped in gloom that gave a vivid effect to the intense sheets of lightning, while the thunder seemed to burst over our very heads, and was reverberated by the groves and forests that checkered and skirted the prairie. Man and beast were so pelted, drenched, and confounded, that the line was thrown in complete confusion; some of the horses were so frightened as to be almost unmanageable, and our scattered cavalcade looked like a tempest-tossed fleet, driven hither and thither, at the mercy of wind and wave.

At length, at half past two o'clock, we came to a halt, and gathering together our forces, encamped in an open and lofty grove, with a prairie on one side and a stream on the other. The forest immediately rang with the sound of the axe, and the crash of falling trees. Huge fires were soon blazing; blankets were stretched before them, by way of tents; booths were hastily reared of bark and skins; every fire had its group drawn close round it, drying and warming themselves, or preparing a comforting meal. Some of the rangers were discharging and cleaning their rifles, which had been exposed to the rain; while the horses, relieved from their saddles and burdens, rolled in the wet grass.

The showers continued from time to time, until late in the evening. Before dark, our horses were gathered in and tethered about the skirts of the camp, within the outposts, through fear of Indian prowlers, who are apt to take advantage of stormy nights for their depredations and assaults. As the night thickened, the huge fires became more and more luminous; lighting up masses of the overhanging foliage, and leaving other parts of the grove in deep gloom. Every fire had its goblin group around it, while the tethered horses were dimly seen, like spectres, among the thickets; excepting that here and there a gray one stood out in bright relief.

The grove, thus fitfully lighted up by the ruddy glare of the fires, resembled a vast leafy dome, walled in by opaque darkness; but every now and then two or three quivering flashes of lightning in quick succession, would suddenly reveal a vast champaign country, where fields and forests, and running streams, would start, as it were, into existence for a few brief seconds, and, before the eye could ascertain them, vanish again into gloom.

A thunder-storm on a prairie, as upon the ocean, derives grandeur and sublimity from the wild and boundless waste over which it rages and bellows. It is not surprising that these awful phenomena of nature should be objects of superstitious reverence to the poor savages, and that they should consider the thunder the angry voice of the Great Spirit. As our half-breeds sat gossiping round the fire, I drew from them some of the notions entertained on the subject by their Indian friends. The latter declare that extinguished thunderbolts are sometimes picked up by hunters on the prairies, who use them for the heads of arrows and lances, and that any warrior thus armed is invincible. Should a thunder-storm occur, however, during battle, he is liable to be carried away by the thunder, and never heard of more.

A warrior of the Konza tribe, hunting on a prairie, was overtaken by a storm, and struck down senseless by the thunder. On recovering, he beheld the thunderbolt lying on the ground, and a horse standing beside it. Snatching up the bolt, he sprang upon the horse, but found, too late, that he was astride of the lightning. In an instant he was whisked away over prairies and forests, and streams and desert, until he was flung senseless at the foot of the Rocky Mountains; whence, on recovering, it took him several months to return to his own people.

This story reminded me of an Indian tradition, related by a traveller, of the fate of a warrior who saw the thunder lying upon the ground, with a beautifully wrought moccason on each side of it. Thinking he had found a prize, he put on the moccasons; but they bore him away to the land of spirits, whence he never returned.

These are simple and artless tales, but they had a wild and romantic interest heard from the lips of half-savage narrators, round a hunter's fire, on a stormy night, with a forest on one side, and a howling waste on the other; and where, peradventure, savage foes might be lurking in the outer darkness.

Our conversation was interrupted by a loud clap of thunder, followed immediately by the sound of a horse galloping off madly into the waste. Every one listened in mute silence. The hoofs resounded vigorously for a time, but grew fainter and fainter, until they died away in remote distance.

When the sound was no longer to be heard, the listeners turned to conjecture what could have caused this sudden scamper. Some thought the horse had been startled by the thunder; others, that some lurking Indian had galloped off with him. To this it was objected, that the usual mode with the Indians is to steal quietly upon the horse, take off his fetters, mount him gently, and walk him off as silently as possible, leading off others, without any unusual stir or noise to disturb the camp.

On the other hand, it was stated as a common practice with the Indians, to creep among a troop of horses when grazing at night, mount one quietly, and then start off suddenly at full speed. Nothing is so contagious among horses as a panic; one sudden break-away of this kind, will sometimes alarm the whole troop, and they will set off, helter-skelter, after the leader.

Every one who had a horse grazing on the skirts of the camp was uneasy, lest his should be the fugitive; but it was impossible to ascertain the fact until morning. Those who had tethered their horses felt more secure; though horses thus tied up, and limited to a short range at night, are apt to fall off in flesh and strength, during a long march;

and many of the horses of the troop already gave signs of being way-worn.

After a gloomy and unruly night, the morning dawned bright and clear, and a glorious sunrise transformed the whole landscape, as if by magic. The late dreary wilderness brightened into a fine open country, with stately groves, and clumps of oaks of a gigantic size, some of which stood singly, as if planted for ornament and shade, in the midst of rich meadows; while our horses, scattered about, and grazing under them, gave to the whole the air of a noble park. It was difficult to realize the fact that we were so far in the wilds beyond the residence of man. Our encampment, alone, had a savage appearance, with its rude tents of skins and blankets, and its columns of blue smoke rising among the trees.

The first care in the morning [October 20], was to look after our horses. Some of them had wandered to a distance, but all were fortunately found; even the one whose clattering hoofs had caused such uneasiness in the night. He had come to a halt about a mile from the camp, and was found quietly grazing near a brook. The bugle sounded for departure about half past eight. As we were in greater risk of Indian molestation the farther we advanced, our line was formed with more precision than heretofore. Every one had his station assigned him, and was forbidden to leave it in pursuit of game, without special permission. The pack-horses were placed in the centre of the line, and a strong guard in the rear.

A Grand Prairie.—Cliff Castle.—Buffalo Tracks.—Deer Hunted by Wolves.—Cross Timber.

AFTER a toilsome march of some distance through a country cut up by ravines and brooks, and entangled by thickets, we emerged upon a grand prairie. Here one of the characteristic scenes of the Far West broke upon us. An immense extent of grassy, undulating, or, as it is termed, rolling country, with here and there a clump of trees, dimly seen in the distance like a ship at sea; the landscape deriving sublimity from its vastness and simplicity. To the southwest, on the summit of a hill, was a singular crest of broken rocks, resembling a ruined fortress. It reminded me of the ruin of some Moorish castle, crowning a height in the midst of a lonely Spanish landscape. To this hill we gave the name of Cliff Castle.[1]

The prairies of these great hunting regions differed in the character of their vegetation from those through which I had hitherto passed. Instead of a profusion of tall flowering plants and long flaunting grasses, they were covered with a shorter growth of herbage called buffalo grass, somewhat coarse, but, at the proper seasons, affording excellent and abundant pasturage. At present it was growing wiry, and in many places was too much parched for grazing.

The weather was verging into that serene but somewhat arid season called the Indian Summer. There was a smoky haze in the atmosphere that tempered the brightness of

[1] Ellsworth wrote that Dr. Holt had named it "Irving's castle" (*Narrative*, 62).

106

the sunshine into a golden tint, softening the features of the landscape, and giving a vagueness to the outlines of distant objects. This haziness was daily increasing, and was attributed to the burning of distant prairies by the Indian hunting parties.

We had not gone far upon the prairie before we came to where deeply-worn footpaths were seen traversing the country: sometimes two or three would keep on parallel to each other, and but a few paces apart. These were pronounced to be traces of buffaloes, where large droves had passed. There were tracks also of horses, which were observed with some attention by our experienced hunters. They could not be the tracks of wild horses, as there were no prints of the hoofs of colts; all were full-grown. As the horses evidently were not shod, it was concluded they must belong to some hunting party of Pawnees. In the course of the morning, the tracks of a single horse, with shoes, were discovered. This might be the horse of a Cherokee hunter, or perhaps a horse stolen from the whites of the frontier. Thus, in traversing these perilous wastes, every foot-print and dint of hoof becomes matter of cautious inspection and shrewd surmise; and the question continually is, whether it be the trace of friend or foe, whether of recent or ancient date, and whether the being that made it be out of reach, or liable to be encountered.

We were getting more and more into the game country: as we proceeded, we repeatedly saw deer to the right and left, bounding off for the coverts; but their appearance no longer excited the same eagerness to pursue. In passing along a slope of the prairie, between two rolling swells of land, we came in sight of a genuine natural hunting match. A pack of seven black wolves and one white one were in full chase of a buck, which they had nearly tired down. They crossed the line of our march without apparently perceiving us; we saw them have a fair run of nearly a mile, gaining upon the buck until they were leaping upon his haunches, when he plunged down a ravine. Some of our party galloped to a rising ground commanding a view of the ravine. The poor buck was completely beset, some on his flanks, some at his throat: he made two or three struggles and desperate bounds, but was dragged down, overpowered, and torn to pieces. The black wolves, in their ravenous hunger and fury, took no notice of the distant group of horsemen; but the white wolf, apparently less game, abandoned the prey, and scampered over hill and dale, rousing various deer that were crouched in the hollows, and which bounded off likewise in different directions. It was altogether a wild scene worthy of the "hunting grounds."

We now came once more in sight of the Red Fork, winding its turbid course between well-wooded hills, and through a vast and magnificent landscape. The prairies bordering on the rivers are always varied in this way with woodland, so beautifully interspersed as to appear to have been laid out by the hand of taste; and they only want here and there a village spire, the battlements of a castle, or the turrets of an old family mansion rising from among the trees, to rival the most ornamented scenery of Europe.

About mid-day we reached the edge of that scattered belt of forest land, about forty miles in width, which stretches across the country from north to south, from the Arkansas to the Red River, separating the upper from the lower prairies, and commonly called the "Cross Timber."[2] On the skirts of this forest land, just on the edge of a prairie, we found traces of a Pawnee encampment of between one and two hundred lodges, showing that the

[2] Their worst troubles with the Cross Timbers do not come until two days later, after they have crossed the Red Fork (Cimarron).

party must have been numerous. The skull of a buffalo lay near the camp, and the moss which had gathered on it proved that the encampment was at least a year old. About half a mile off we encamped in a beautiful grove, watered by a fine spring and rivulet. Our day's journey had been about fourteen miles.

In the course of the afternoon we were rejoined by two of Lieutenant King's[3] party, which we had left behind a few days before, to look after stray horses. All the horses had been found, though some had wandered to the distance of several miles. The lieutenant, with seventeen of his companions, had remained at our last night's encampment to hunt, having come upon recent traces of buffalo. They had also seen a fine wild horse, which, however, had galloped off with a speed that defied pursuit.

Confident anticipations were now indulged, that on the following day we should meet with buffalo, and perhaps with wild horses, and every one was in spirits. We needed some excitement of the kind, for our young men were growing weary of marching and encamping under restraint, and provisions this day were scanty. The Captain and several of the rangers went out hunting, but brought home nothing but a small deer and a few turkeys. Our two men, Beatte and Tonish, likewise went out. The former returned with a deer athwart his horse, which, as usual, he laid down by our lodge, and said nothing. Tonish returned with no game, but with his customary budget of wonderful tales. Both he and the deer had done marvels. Not one had come within the lure of his rifle without being hit in a mortal part, yet, strange to say, every one had kept on his way without flinching. We all determined that, from the accuracy of his aim, Tonish must have shot with

[3] Robert King, second lieutenant (*Western Journals*, 181). Ellsworth did not find King a very soldierly officer (*Narrative*, 24).

charmed balls, but that every deer had a charmed life. The most important intelligence brought by him, however, was, that he had seen the fresh tracks of several wild horses. He now considered himself upon the eve of great exploits, for there was nothing upon which he glorified himself more than his skill in horse-catching.

OCT. 21. This morning the camp was in a bustle at an early hour: the expectation of falling in with buffalo in the course of the day roused every one's spirit. There was a continual cracking of rifles, that they might be reloaded: the shot was drawn off from double-barrelled guns, and balls were substituted. Tonish, however, prepared chiefly for a campaign against wild horses. He took the field, with a coil of cordage hung at his saddle-bow, and a couple of white wands, something like fishing-rods, eight or ten feet in length, with forked ends. The coil of cordage thus used in hunting the wild horse, is called a lariat, and answers to the lasso of South America. It is not flung, however, in the graceful and dexterous Spanish style. The hunter, after a hard chase, when he succeeds in getting almost head and head with the wild horse, hitches the running noose of the lariat over his head by means of the forked stick; then letting him have the full length of the cord, plays him like a fish, and chokes him into subjection.

All this Tonish promised to exemplify to our full satisfaction; we had not much confidence in his success, and feared he might knock up a good horse in a headlong gallop after a bad one: for, like all the French creoles, he was a merciless hard rider. It was determined, therefore, to keep a sharp eye upon him, and to check his sallying propensities.

We had not proceeded far on our morning's march, when we were checked by a deep stream, running along the bottom of a thickly-wooded ravine. After coasting it for a couple of miles, we came to a fording place; but to get down to it was the difficulty, for the banks were steep and crumbling, and overgrown with forest trees, mingled with thickets, brambles, and grape-vines. At length the leading horseman broke his way through the thicket, and his horse, putting his feet together, slid down the black crumbling bank, to the narrow margin of the stream; then floundering across, with mud and water up to the saddle-girths, he scrambled up on the opposite bank, and arrived safe on level ground. The whole line followed pell-mell after the leader, and pushing forward in close order, Indian file, they crowded each other down the bank and into the stream. Some of the horsemen missed the ford, and were soused over head and ears; one was unhorsed, and plumped head foremost into the middle of the stream: for my own part, while pressed forward, and hurried over the bank by those behind me, I was interrupted by a grape-vine, as thick as a cable, which hung in a festoon as low as the saddle-bow, and, dragging me from the saddle, threw me among the feet of the trampling horses. Fortunately, I escaped without injury, regained my steed, crossed the stream without further difficulty, and was enabled to join in the merriment occasioned by the ludicrous disasters of the fording.

It is at passes like this that occur the most dangerous ambuscades and sanguinary surprises of Indian warfare. A party of savages well placed among the thickets might have made sad havoc among our men, while entangled in the ravine.

We now came out upon a vast and glorious prairie, spreading out beneath the golden beams of an autumnal sun. The deep and frequent traces of buffalo, showed it to be one of their favorite grazing grounds; yet none were to be seen. In the course of the morning, we were over-taken by the lieutenant and seventeen men, who had re-mained behind, and who came laden with the spoils of buffaloes; having killed three on the preceding day. One of the rangers, however, had little luck to boast of; his horse having taken fright at sight of the buffaloes, thrown his rider, and escaped into the woods.

The excitement of our hunters, both young and old, now rose almost to fever height; scarce any of them hav-ing ever encountered any of this far-famed game of the prairies. Accordingly, when in the course of the day the cry of buffalo! buffalo! rose from one part of the line, the whole troop were thrown in agitation. We were just then passing through a beautiful part of the prairie, finely di-versified by hills and slopes, and woody dells, and high stately groves. Those who had given the alarm, pointed out a large black-looking animal, slowly moving along the side of a rising ground, about two miles off. The ever-ready Tonish jumped up, and stood with his feet on the saddle, and his forked stick in his hands, like a posture-master of scaramouch at a circus, just ready for a feat of horsemanship. After gazing at the animal for a moment, which he could have seen full as well without rising from his stirrups, he pronounced it a wild horse; and dropping again into his saddle, was about to dash off full tilt in pur-suit, when, to his inexpressible chagrin, he was called back, and ordered to keep to his post, in rear of the baggage horses.

The Captain and two of his officers now set off to recon-noitre the game. It was the intention of the Captain, who was an admirable marksman, to endeavor to crease the horse; that is to say, to hit him with a rifle ball in the ridge of the neck. A wound of this kind paralyzes a horse for a moment; he falls to the ground, and may be secured before he recovers. It is a cruel expedient, however, for an ill-directed shot may kill or maim the noble animal.

As the Captain and his companions moved off laterally and slowly, in the direction of the horse, we continued our course forward; watching intently, however, the movements of the game. The horse moved quietly over the profile of the rising ground, and disappeared behind it. The Captain and his party were likewise soon hidden by an intervening hill.

After a time, the horse suddenly made his appearance to our right, just ahead of the line, emerging out of a small valley, on a brisk trot; having evidently taken the alarm. At sight of us he stopped short, gazed at us for an instant with surprise, then tossing up his head, trotted off in fine style, glancing at us first over one shoulder, then over the other, his ample mane and tail streaming in the wind. Having dashed through a skirt of thicket, that looked like a hedge-row, he paused in the open field beyond, glanced back at us again, with a beautiful bend of the neck, snuffed the air, then tossing his head again, broke into a gallop, and took refuge in a wood.

It was the first time I had ever seen a horse scouring his native wilderness in all the pride and freedom of his nature. How different from the poor, mutilated, harnessed, checked, reined-up victim of luxury, caprice, and avarice, in our cities!

After travelling about fifteen miles, we encamped about one o'clock, that our hunters might have time to procure a supply of provisions. Our encampment was in a spacious grove of lofty oaks and walnuts, free from underwood, on the border of a brook. While unloading the pack-horses, our little Frenchman was loud in his complaints at having been prevented from pursuing the wild horse, which he would certainly have taken. In the meantime, I saw our half-breed, Beatte, quietly saddle his best horse, a powerful steed of half savage race, hang a lariat at the saddle-bow, take a rifle and forked stick in hand, and, mounting, depart from the camp without saying a word. It was evident he was going off in quest of the wild horse, but was disposed to hunt alone.

✌➢ XX ⟨➢

The Camp of the Wild Horse.
Hunters' Stories.—Habits of the Wild Horse.—The Half-
breed and the Prize.—A Horse Chase.—A Wild Spirit
Tamed.

WE HAD ENCAMPED in a good neighborhood for
game, as the reports of rifles in various directions speedily
gave notice. One of our hunters soon returned with the
meat of a doe, tied up in the skin, and slung across his
shoulders. Another brought a fat buck across his horse.
Two other deer were brought in, and a number of turkeys.
All the game was thrown down in front of the Captain's
fire, to be portioned out among the various messes. The
spits and camp-kettles were soon in full employ, and
throughout the evening there was a scene of hunters' feasting and profusion.

We had been disappointed this day in our hopes of
meeting with buffalo, but the sight of the wild horse had
been a great novelty, and gave a turn to the conversation
of the camp for the evening. There were several anecdotes
told of a famous gray horse, which has ranged the prairies
of this neighborhood for six or seven years, setting at
naught every attempt of the hunters to capture him. They
say he can pace and rack (or amble) faster than the fleetest
horses can run. Equally marvellous accounts were given
of a black horse on the Brazos, who grazed the prairies
on that river's banks in Texas. For years he outstripped
all pursuit. His fame spread far and wide; offers were made
for him to the amount of a thousand dollars; the boldest
and most hard-riding hunters tried incessantly to make
prize of him, but in vain. At length he fell a victim to his
gallantry, being decoyed under a tree by a tame mare, and

a noose dropped over his head by a boy perched among the branches.

The capture of the wild horse is one of the most favorite achievements of the prairie tribes; and, indeed, it is from this source that the Indian hunters chiefly supply themselves. The wild horses which range those vast grassy plains, extending from the Arkansas to the Spanish settlements, are of various forms and colors, betraying their various descents. Some resemble the common English stock, and are probably descended from horses which have escaped from our border settlements. Others are of a low but strong make, and are supposed to be of the Andalusian breed, brought out by the Spanish discoverers.

Some fanciful speculatists have seen in them descendants of the Arab stock, brought into Spain from Africa, and thence transferred to this country; and have pleased themselves with the idea, that their sires may have been of the pure coursers of the desert, that once bore Mahomet and his warlike disciples across the sandy plains of Arabia.

The habits of the Arab seem to have come with the steed. The introduction of the horse on the boundless prairies of the Far West changed the whole mode of living of their inhabitants. It gave them that facility of rapid motion, and of sudden and distant change of place, so dear to the roving propensities of man. Instead of lurking in the depths of gloomy forests, and patiently threading the mazes of a tangled wilderness on foot, like his brethren of the north, the Indian of the West is a rover of the plain; he leads a brighter and more sunshiny life; almost always on horseback, on vast flowery prairies and under cloudless skies.

I was lying by the Captain's fire, late in the evening, listening to stories about those coursers of the prairies, and weaving speculations of my own, when there was a clamor of voices and a loud cheering at the other end of the camp; and word was passed that Beatte, the half-breed, had brought in a wild horse.

In an instant every fire was deserted; the whole camp crowded to see the Indian and his prize. It was a colt about two years old, well grown, finely limbed, with bright prominent eyes, and a spirited yet gentle demeanor. He gazed about him with an air of mingled stupefaction and surprise, at the men, the horses, and the camp-fires; while the Indian stood before him with folded arms, having hold of the other end of the cord which noosed his captive, and gazing on him with a most imperturbable aspect. Beatte, as I have before observed, has a greenish olive complexion, with a strongly marked countenance, not unlike the bronze casts of Napoleon; and as he stood before his captive horse, with folded arms and fixed aspect, he looked more like a statue than a man.

If the horse, however, manifested the least restiveness, Beatte would immediately worry him with the lariat, jerking him first on one side, then on the other, so as almost to throw him on the ground; when he had thus rendered him passive, he would resume his statue-like attitude and gaze at him in silence.

The whole scene was singularly wild; the tall grove, partially illumined by the flashing fires of the camp, the horses tethered here and there among the trees, the carcasses of deer hanging around, and in the midst of all, the wild huntsman and his wild horse, with an admiring throng of rangers, almost as wild.

In the eagerness of their excitement, several of the young rangers sought to get the horse by purchase or barter, and even offered extravagant terms; but Beatte declined all their offers. "You give great price now"; said he, "to-morrow you be sorry, and take back, and say d——d Indian!"

The young men importuned him with questions about the mode in which he took the horse, but his answers were dry and laconic; he evidently retained some pique at having been undervalued and sneered at by them; and at the same time looked down upon them with contempt as greenhorns, little versed in the noble science of woodcraft.

Afterward, however, when he was seated by our fire, I readily drew from him an account of his exploit; for, though taciturn among strangers, and little prone to boast of his actions, yet his taciturnity, like that of all Indians, had its times of relaxation.

He informed me, that on leaving the camp, he had returned to the place where we had lost sight of the wild horse. Soon getting upon its track, he followed it to the banks of the river. Here, the prints being more distinct in the sand, he perceived that one of the hoofs was broken and defective, so he gave up the pursuit.

As he was returning to the camp, he came upon a gang of six horses, which immediately made for the river. He pursued them across the stream, left his rifle on the river bank, and putting his horse to full speed, soon came up with the fugitives. He attempted to noose one of them, but the lariat hitched on one of his ears, and he shook it off. The horses dashed up a hill, he followed hard at their heels, when, of a sudden, he saw their tails whisking in the air, and they plunging down a precipice. It was too late to stop. He shut his eyes, held in his breath, and went over with them—neck or nothing. The descent was between twenty and thirty feet, but they all came down safe upon a sandy bottom.

He now succeeded in throwing his noose round a fine young horse. As he galloped alongside of him, the two horses passed each side of a sapling, and the end of the lariat was jerked out of his hand. He regained it, but an intervening tree obliged him again to let it go. Having once more caught it, and coming to a more open country, he was enabled to play the young horse with the line until he gradually checked and subdued him, so as to lead him to the place where he had left his rifle.

He had another formidable difficulty in getting him across the river, where both horses stuck for a time in the mire, and Beatte was nearly unseated from his saddle by the force of the current and the struggle of his captive. After much toil and trouble, however, he got across the stream, and brought his prize safe into camp.

For the remainder of the evening, the camp remained in a high state of excitement; nothing was talked of but the capture of wild horses; every youngster of the troop was for this harum-scarum kind of chase; every one promised himself to return from the campaign in triumph, bestriding one of these wild coursers of the prairies. Beatte had suddenly risen to great importance; he was the prime hunter, the hero of the day. Offers were made him by the best mounted rangers, to let him ride their horses in the chase, provided he would give them a share of the spoil. Beatte bore his honors in silence, and closed with none of the offers. Our stammering, chattering, gasconading little Frenchman, however, made up for his taciturnity, by vaunting as much upon the subject as if it were he that had caught the horse. Indeed he held forth so learnedly in the matter, and boasted so much of the many horses he had taken, that he began to be considered an oracle; and some of the youngsters were inclined to doubt whether he were not superior even to the taciturn Beatte.

The excitement kept the camp awake later than usual. The hum of voices, interrupted by occasional peals of laughter, was heard from the groups around the various fires, and the night was considerably advanced before all had sunk to sleep.

With the morning dawn the excitement revived, and Beatte and his wild horse were again the gaze and talk of the camp. The captive had been tied all night to a tree among the other horses. He was again led forth by Beatte, by a long halter or lariat, and, on his manifesting the least restiveness, was, as before, jerked and worried into passive submission. He appeared to be gentle and docile by nature, and had a beautifully mild expression of the eye. In his strange and forlorn situation, the poor animal seemed to seek protection and companionship in the very horse which had aided to capture him.

Seeing him thus gentle and tractable, Beatte, just as we were about to march, strapped a light pack upon his back, by way of giving him the first lesson in servitude. The native pride and independence of the animal took fire at this indignity. He reared, and plunged, and kicked, and tried in every way to get rid of the degrading burden. The Indian was too potent for him. At every paroxysm he renewed the discipline of the halter, until the poor animal, driven to despair, threw himself prostrate on the ground, and lay motionless, as if acknowledging himself vanquished. A stage hero, representing the despair of a captive prince, could not have played his part more dramatically. There was absolutely a moral grandeur in it.

The imperturbable Beatte folded his arms, and stood for a time, looking down in silence upon his captive; until seeing him perfectly subdued, he nodded his head slowly, screwed his mouth into a sardonic smile of triumph, and, with a jerk of the halter, ordered him to rise. He obeyed, and from that time forward offered no resistance. During that day he bore his pack patiently, and was led by the halter; but in two days he followed voluntarily at large among the supernumerary horses of the troop.

I could not but look with compassion upon this fine young animal, whose whole course of existence had been so suddenly reversed. From being a denizen of these vast pastures, ranging at will from plain to plain and mead to mead, cropping of every herb and flower, and drinking of every stream, he was suddenly reduced to perpetual and painful servitude, to pass his life under the harness and the curb, amid, perhaps, the din and dust and drudgery of cities. The transition in his lot was such as sometimes takes place in human affairs, and in the fortunes of towering individuals:—one day, a prince of the prairies—the next day, a pack-horse![1]

[1] Ellsworth also described this episode at considerable length (*Narrative*, 89–91).

The Fording of the Red Fork.—The Dreary Forests of the
"Cross Timber."—Buffalo!

WE LEFT THE CAMP of the wild horse about a quarter before eight [October 22], and, after steering nearly
south for three or four miles, arrived on the banks of the
Red Fork, about seventy-five miles, as we supposed, above
its mouth. The river was about three hundred yards wide,
wandering among sand-bars and shoals. Its shores, and the
long sandy banks that stretched out into the stream, were
printed, as usual, with the traces of various animals that
had come down to cross it, or to drink its waters.

Here we came to a halt, and there was much consultation about the possibility of fording the river with safety,
as there was an apprehension of quicksands. Beatte, who
had been somewhat in the rear, came up while we were
debating. He was mounted on his horse of the half-wild
breed, and leading his captive by the bridle. He gave the
latter in charge to Tonish, and without saying a word,
urged his horse into the stream, and crossed it safely.
Everything was done by this man in a similar way, promptly, resolutely, and silently, without a previous promise or
an after vaunt.

The troop now followed the lead of Beatte, and reached
the opposite shore without any mishap, though one of the
pack-horses wandered a little from the track, came near
being swallowed up in a quicksand, and was with difficulty
dragged to land.

After crossing the river, we had to force our way, for
nearly a mile, through a thick canebrake, which, at first

sight, appeared an impervious mass of reeds and brambles. It was a hard struggle; our horses were often to the saddle-girths in mire and water, and both horse and horseman harassed and torn by bush and brier. Falling, however, upon a buffalo track, we at length extricated ourselves from this morass, and ascended a ridge of land, where we beheld a beautiful open country before us; while to our right, the belt of forest land, called "The Cross Timber," continued stretching away to the southward, as far as the eye could reach. We soon abandoned the open country, and struck into the forest land. It was the intention of the Captain to keep on southwest by south, and traverse the Cross Timber diagonally, so as to come out upon the edge of the great western prairie. By thus maintaining something of a southerly direction, he trusted, while he crossed the belt of the forest, he would at the same time approach the Red River.

The plan of the Captain was judicious; but he erred from not being informed of the nature of the country. Had he kept directly west, a couple of days would have carried us through the forest land, and we might then have had an easy course along the skirts of the upper prairies, to Red River; by going diagonally, we were kept for many weary days toiling through a dismal series of rugged forests.

The Cross Timber is about forty miles in breadth, and stretches over a rough country of rolling hills, covered with scattered tracts of post-oak and black-jack; with some intervening valleys, which, at proper seasons, would afford good pasturage. It is very much cut up by deep ravines, which, in the rainy seasons, are the beds of temporary streams, tributary to the main rivers, and these are called "branches." The whole tract may present a pleasant aspect in the fresh time of the year, when the ground is covered with herbage; when the trees are in their green leaf, and the glens are enlivened by running streams. Unfortunately, we entered it too late in the season. The herbage was parched; the foliage of the scrubby forests was withered; the whole woodland prospect, as far as the eye could reach, had a brown and arid hue. The fires made on the prairies by the Indian hunters, had frequently penetrated these forests, sweeping in light transient flames along the dry grass, scorching and calcining the lower twigs and branches of the trees, and leaving them black and hard, so as to tear the flesh of man and horse that had to scramble through them. I shall not easily forget the mortal toil, and the vexations of flesh and spirit, that we underwent occasionally, in our wanderings through the Cross Timber. It was like struggling through forests of cast iron.[1]

After a tedious ride of several miles, we came out upon an open tract of hill and dale, interspersed with woodland. Here we were roused by the cry of buffalo! buffalo! The effect was something like that of the cry of a sail! a sail! at sea. It was not a false alarm. Three or four of those enormous animals were visible to our sight grazing on the slope of a distant hill.

There was a general movement to set off in pursuit, and it was with some difficulty that the vivacity of the younger

[1] Ellsworth described the difficulty of passage through the Cross Timbers in his entry for October 21, before they had crossed the Red Fork (Cimarron); possibly he was writing a day or two later. "I never saw a man more impatient, to be out of them, than Mr Irving—and well he might complain. He had nothing but cloth gloves to defend his hands—His frock surtout, was in a moment, shorn of its beauty and use. While, he was passing through what he called the cast iron stuff, protecting his head, & eyes, and cap (which was knocked off several times every day) the whole of one skirt of his coat was taken off, and done so expertly, that he never knew it at the time" (*Narrative*, 88). On October 22, they were still struggling through the "cast iron black jack" (*ibid.*, 92).

men of the troop could be restrained. Leaving orders that the line of march should be preserved, the Captain and two of his officers departed at a quiet pace, accompanied by Beatte, and by the ever-forward Tonish; for it was impossible any longer to keep the little Frenchman in check, being half crazy to prove his skill and prowess in hunting the buffalo.

The intervening hills soon hid from us both the game and the huntsmen. We kept on our course in quest of a camping-place, which was difficult to be found; almost all the channels of the streams being dry, and the country being destitute of fountain heads.

After proceeding some distance, there was again a cry of buffalo, and two were pointed out on a hill to the left. The Captain being absent, it was no longer possible to restrain the ardor of the young hunters. Away several of them dashed, full speed, and soon disappeared among the ravines: the rest kept on, anxious to find a proper place for encampment.

Indeed we now began to experience the disadvantages of the season. The pasturage of the prairies was scanty and parched: the pea-vines which grew in the woody bottoms were withered, and most of the "branches" or streams were dried up. While wandering in this perplexity, we were overtaken by the Captain and all his party, except Tonish. They had pursued the buffalo for some distance without getting within shot, and had given up the chase, being fearful of fatiguing their horses, or being led off too far from camp. The little Frenchman, however, had galloped after them like mad, and the last they saw of him, he was engaged, as it were, yard-arm and yard-arm, with a great buffalo bull, firing broadsides into him. "I tink dat little man crazy—somehow," observed Beatte, dryly.

The Alarm Camp.

We now came to a halt, and had to content ourselves with an indifferent encampment. It was in a grove of scrub-oaks, on the borders of a deep ravine, at the bottom of which were a few scanty pools of water. We were just at the foot of a gradually-sloping hill, covered with half-withered grass, that afforded meagre pasturage. In the spot where we had encamped, the grass was high and parched. The view around us was circumscribed and much shut in by gently-swelling hills.

Just as we were encamping, Tonish arrived, all glorious, from his hunting match; his white horse hung all around with buffalo meat. According to his own account, he had laid low two mighty bulls. As usual, we deducted one half from his boastings; but, now that he had something real to vaunt about, there was no restraining the valor of his tongue.[1]

After having in some measure appeased his vanity by boasting of his exploit, he informed us that he had observed the fresh track of horses, which, from various circumstances, he suspected to have been made by some roving band of Pawnees. This caused some little uneasiness. The young men who had left the line of march in pursuit of the two buffaloes, had not yet rejoined us; apprehensions were expressed that they might be waylaid and attacked. Our veteran hunter, old Ryan, also, immediately on our halting to encamp, had gone off on foot, in company with

[1] Ellsworth credited him with two (*Narrative*, 92).

a young disciple. "Dat old man will have his brains knocked out by de Pawnee yet," said Beatte. "He tink he know every ting, but he don't know Pawnees, anyhow."

Taking his rifle, the Captain repaired on foot to reconnoitre the country from the naked summit of one of the neighboring hills. In the meantime, the horses were hobbled and turned loose to graze; and wood was cut, and fires made, to prepare the evening's repast.

Suddenly there was an alarm of fire in the camp! The flame from one of the kindling fires had caught to the tall dry grass: a breeze was blowing; there was danger that the camp would soon be wrapped in a light blaze. "Look to the horses!" cried one; "Drag away the baggage!" cried another. "Take care of the rifles and powder-horns!" cried a third. All was hurry-scurry and uproar. The horses dashed wildly about: some of the men snatched away rifles and powder-horns, others dragged off saddles and saddle-bags. Meantime, no one thought of quelling the fire, nor indeed knew how to quell it. Beatte, however, and his comrades attacked it in the Indian mode, beating down the edges of the fire with blankets and horse-cloths, and endeavoring to prevent its spreading among the grass; the rangers followed their example, and in a little while the flames were happily quelled.

The fires were now properly kindled on places from whence the dry grass had been cleared away. The horses were scattered about a small valley, and on the sloping hillside, cropping the scanty herbage. Tonish was preparing a sumptuous evening's meal from his buffalo meat, promising us a rich soup and a prime piece of roast beef: but we were doomed to experience another and more serious alarm.

There was an indistinct cry from some rangers on the

summit of the hill, of which we could only distinguish the words, "The horses! the horses! get in the horses!"

Immediately a clamor of voices arose; shouts, inquiries, replies, were all mingled together, so that nothing could be clearly understood, and everyone drew his own inference.

"The Captain has started buffaloes," cried one, "and wants horses for the chase." Immediately a number of rangers seized their rifles, and scampered for the hill-top. "The prairie is on fire beyond the hill," cried another, "I see the smoke—the Captain means we shall drive the horses beyond the brook."

By this time a ranger from the hill had reached the skirts of the camp. He was almost breathless, and could only say that the Captain had seen Indians at a distance.

"Pawnees! Pawnees!" was now the cry among our wild-headed youngsters. "Drive the horses into the camp!" cried one. "Saddle the horses!" cried another. "Form the line!" cried a third. There was now a scene of clamor and confusion that baffles all description. The rangers were scampering about the adjacent field in pursuit of their horses. One might be seen tugging his steed along by a halter; another without a hat, riding bare-backed; another driving a hobbled horse before him, that made awkward leaps like a kangaroo.

The alarm increased. Word was brought from the lower end of the camp that there was a band of Pawnees in a neighboring valley. They had shot old Ryan through the head, and were chasing his companion! "No, it was not old Ryan that was killed—it was one of the hunters that had been after the two buffaloes." "There are three hundred Pawnees just beyond the hill," cried one voice. "More, more!" cried another.

Our situation, shut in among hills, prevented our seeing
to any distance, and left us a prey to all these rumors. A
cruel enemy was supposed to be at hand, and an immediate attack apprehended. The horses by this time were
driven into the camp, and were dashing about among the
fires, and trampling upon the baggage. Every one endeavored to prepare for action; but here was the perplexity. During the late alarm of fire, the saddles, bridles, rifles,
powder-horns, and other equipments, had been snatched
out of their places, and thrown helter-skelter among the
trees.

"Where is my saddle?" cried one. "Has any one seen
my rifle?" cried another. "Who will lend me a ball?" cried
a third, who was loading his piece. "I have lost my bullet-
pouch." "For God's sake help me to girth this horse!"
cried another; "he's so restive I can do nothing with him."
In his hurry and worry, he had put on the saddle the hind
part before![2]

Some affected to swagger and talk bold; others said
nothing, but went on steadily, preparing their horses and
weapons, and on these I felt the most reliance. Some were
evidently excited and elated with the idea of an encounter
with Indians; and none more so than my young Swiss
fellow-traveller, who had a passion for wild adventure.
Our man, Beatte, led his horses in the rear of the camp,

[2] Irving was not so calm as he sounds, if we are to believe Ellsworth: "Mr Irving could find only one *Leggin,* and he was calling
through the camp loud and louder still, for his odd leggin, of mighty
little consequence in a battle—He was as *pale* as he could be, and
much terrified—" It was Latrobe who put his saddle on "wrong side
before and girted it in this manner." Pourtalès may have been excited with the adventure, but the Commissioner credited him with
one of the more reasonable statements: "whether it was best to take
saddle bags or not?" (*Narrative,* 93). The Commissioner, of course,
remained entirely cool and collected.

placed his rifle against a tree, then seated himself by the fire in perfect silence. On the other hand, little Tonish, who was busy cooking, stopped every moment from his work to play the fanfaron, singing, swearing, and affecting an unusual hilarity, which made me strongly suspect there was some little fright at bottom, to cause all this effervescence.

About a dozen of the rangers, as soon as they could saddle their horses, dashed off in the direction in which the Pawnees were said to have attacked the hunters. It was now determined, in case our camp should be assailed, to put our horses in the ravine in the rear, where they would be out of danger from arrow or rifle ball, and to take our stand within the edge of the ravine. This would serve as a trench, and the trees and thickets with which it was bordered, would be sufficient to turn aside any shaft of the enemy. The Pawnees, besides, are wary of attacking any covert of any kind; their warfare, as I have already observed, lies in the open prairie, where, mounted upon their fleet horses, they can swoop like hawks upon their enemy, or wheel about him and discharge their arrows. Still I could not but perceive, that, in case of being attacked by such a number of these well-mounted and warlike savages as were said to be at hand, we should be exposed to considerable risk from the inexperience and want of discipline of our newly-raised rangers, and from the very courage of many of the younger ones who seemed bent on adventure and exploit.

By this time the Captain reached the camp, and every one crowded round him for information. He informed us, that he had proceeded some distance on his reconnoitering expedition, and was slowly returning toward the camp, along the brow of a naked hill, when he saw something on the edge of a parallel hill, that looked like a man. He paused, and watched it; but it remained so perfectly motionless, that he supposed it a bush, or the top of some tree beyond the hill. He resumed his course, when it likewise began to move in a parallel direction. Another form now rose beside it, of some one who had either been lying down, or had just ascended the other side of the hill. The Captain stopped and regarded them; they likewise stopped. He then lay down upon the grass, and they began to walk. On his rising, they again stopped, as if watching him. Knowing that the Indians were apt to have their spies and sentinels thus posted on the summit of naked hills, commanding extensive prospects, his doubts were increased by the suspicious movements of these men. He now put his foraging cap on the end of his rifle, and waived it in the air. They took no notice of the signal. He then walked on, until he entered the edge of a wood, which concealed him from their view. Stopping out of sight for a moment, he again looked forth, when he saw the two men passing swiftly forward. As the hill on which they were walking made a curve toward that on which he stood, it seemed as if they were endeavoring to head him before he should reach the camp. Doubting whether they might not belong to some large party of Indians, either in ambush or moving along the valley beyond the hill, the Captain hastened his steps homeward, and, descrying some rangers on an eminence between him and the camp, he called out to them to pass the word to have the horses driven in, as these are generally the first objects of Indian depredation.

Such was the origin of the alarm which had thrown the camp in commotion. Some of those who heard the Captain's narration, had no doubt that the men on the hill were Pawnee scouts, belonging to the band that had waylaid the hunters. Distant shots were heard at intervals, which were supposed to be fired by those who had sallied out to rescue their comrades. Several more rangers, having completed their equipments, now rode forth in the direction of the firing; others looked anxious and uneasy.

"If they are as numerous as they are said to be," said one, "and as well mounted as they generally are, we shall be a bad match for them with our jaded horses."

"Well," replied the Captain, "we have a strong encampment, and can stand a siege."

"Ay, but they may set fire to the prairie in the night, and burn us out of our encampment."

"We will then set up a counter-fire!"

The word was now passed that a man on horseback approached the camp.

"It is one of the hunters! It is Clements![3] He brings buffalo meat!" was announced by several voices as the horseman drew near.

It was, in fact, one of the rangers who had set off in the morning in pursuit of the two buffaloes. He rode into camp, with the spoils of the chase hanging round his horse, and followed by his companions, all sound and unharmed, and equally well laden. They proceeded to give an account of a grand gallop they had had after the two buffaloes, and how many shots it had cost them to bring one to the ground.

"Well, but the Pawnees—the Pawnees—where are the Pawnees?"

"What Pawnees?"

"The Pawnees that attacked you."

"No one attacked us."

"But have you seen no Indians on your way?"

"Oh yes, two of us got to the top of a hill to look out for the camp, and saw a fellow on an opposite hill cutting queer antics, who seemed to be an Indian."

[3] Jeremiah C. Clements, of Batesville (*Western Journals*, 182).

"Pshaw! that was I!" said the Captain.

Here the bubble burst. The whole alarm had risen from this mutual mistake of the Captain and the two rangers. As to the report of the three hundred Pawnees and their attack on the hunters, it proved to be a wanton fabrication, of which no further notice was taken; though the author deserved to have been sought out, and severely punished.

There being no longer any prospect of fighting, every one now thought of eating; and here the stomachs throughout the camp were in unison. Tonish served up to us his promised regale of buffalo soup and buffalo meat. The soup was peppered most horribly, and the roast beef proved the bull to have been one of the patriarchs of the prairies; never did I have to deal with a tougher morsel. However, it was our first repast on buffalo meat, so we ate it with a lively faith; nor would our little Frenchman allow us any rest, until he had extorted from us an acknowledgment of the excellence of his cookery; though the pepper gave us the lie in our throats.

The night closed in without the return of old Ryan and his companion. We had become accustomed, however, to the aberrations of this old cock of the woods, and no further solicitude was expressed on his account.

After the fatigues and agitations of the day, the camp soon sunk into a profound sleep, excepting those on guard, who were more than usually on the alert; for the traces recently seen of Pawnees, and the certainty that we were in the midst of their hunting grounds, excited to constant vigilance. About half past ten o'clock we were all startled from sleep, by a new alarm. A sentinel had fired off his rifle and run into camp, crying that there were Indians at hand.

Every one was on his legs in an instant. Some seized

their rifles; some were about to saddle their horses; some hastened to the Captain's lodge, but were ordered back to their respective fires. The sentinel was examined. He declared he had seen an Indian approach, crawling along the ground; whereupon he had fired upon him, and run into camp. The Captain gave it as his opinion, that the supposed Indian was a wolf; he reprimanded the sentinel for deserting his post, and obliged him to return to it. Many seemed inclined to give credit to the story of the sentinel; for the events of the day had predisposed them to apprehend lurking foes and sudden assaults during the darkness of the night. For a long time they sat round their fires, with rifle in hand, carrying on low, murmuring conversations, and listening for some new alarm. Nothing further, however, occurred; the voices gradually died away; the gossipers nodded and dozed, and sunk to rest; and, by degrees, silence and sleep once more stole over the camp.

◄§ XXIII §►

*Beaver Dam.—Buffalo and Horse Tracks.—A Pawnee Trail.
—Wild Horses.—The Young Hunter and the Bear.—
Change of Route.*

O N MUSTERING our forces in the morning, (Oct. 23,)
old Ryan and his comrades were still missing; but the Captain had such perfect reliance on the skill and resources
of the veteran woodsman, that he did not think it necessary to take any measures with respect to him.

Our march this day lay through the same kind of rough
rolling country; checkered by brown dreary forests of
post-oak, and cut up by deep dry ravines. The distant fires
were evidently increasing on the prairies. The wind had
been at northwest for several days; and the atmosphere
had become so smoky, as in the height of Indian summer,
that it was difficult to distinguish objects at any distance.

In the course of the morning, we crossed a deep stream
with a complete beaver dam, above three feet high, making a large pond, and doubtless containing several families
of that industrious animal, though not one showed his nose
above water. The Captain would not permit this amphib-
ious commonwealth to be disturbed.

We were now continually coming upon the tracks of
buffaloes and wild horses; those of the former tended in-
variably to the south, as we could perceive by the direction of the trampled grass. It was evident we were on the
great highway of these migratory herds, but that they
had chiefly passed to the southward.

Beatte, who generally kept a parallel course several hundred yards distant from our line of march, to be on the
look-out for game, and who regarded every track with the

knowing eye of an Indian, reported that he had come upon a very suspicious trail. There were the tracks of men who wore Pawnee moccasons. He had scented the smoke of mingled sumach and tobacco, such as the Indians use. He had observed tracks of horses, mingled with those of a dog; and a mark in the dust where a cord had been trailed along; probably the long bridle, one end of which the Indian horsemen suffer to trail on the ground. It was evident, they were not the tracks of wild horses. My anxiety began to revive about the safety of our veteran hunter Ryan, for I had taken a great fancy to this real old Leatherstocking; every one expressed a confidence, however, that wherever Ryan was, he was safe, and knew how to take care of himself.

We had accomplished the greater part of a weary day's march, and were passing through a glade of the oak openings, when we came in sight of six wild horses, among which I especially noticed two very handsome ones, a gray and a roan. They pranced about, with heads erect, and long flaunting tails, offering a proud contrast to our poor, spiritless, travel-tired steeds. Having reconnoitered us for a moment, they set off at a gallop, passed through a woody dingle, and in a little while emerged once more to view, trotting up a slope about a mile distant.

The sight of these horses was again a sore trial to the vaporing Tonish, who had his lariat and forked stick ready, and was on the point of launching forth in pursuit, on his jaded horse, when he was again ordered back to the packhorses. After a day's journey of fourteen miles in a southwest direction, we encamped on the banks of a small clear stream, on the northern border of the Cross Timber;[1] and on the edge of those vast prairies, that extend away to the

[1] Hardly on the "northern" border. They had reached the Cross Timbers on October 20, two days before crossing the Red Fork.

foot of the Rocky Mountains. In turning loose the horses to graze, their bells were stuffed with grass to prevent their tinkling, lest it might be heard by some wandering horde of Pawnees.

Our hunters now went out in different directions, but without much success, as but one deer was brought into the camp. A young ranger had a long story to tell of his adventures. In skirting the thickets of a deep ravine he had wounded a buck, which he plainly heard to fall among the bushes. He stopped to fix the lock of his rifle, which was out of order, and to reload it: then advancing to the edge of the thicket, in quest of his game, he heard a low growling. Putting the branches aside, and stealing silently forward, he looked down into the ravine and beheld a huge bear dragging the carcass of the deer along the dry channel of a brook, and growling and snarling at four or five officious wolves, who seemed to have dropped in to take supper with him.

The ranger fired at the bear, but missed him. Bruin maintained his ground and his prize, and seemed disposed to make battle. The wolves, too, who were evidently sharp set, drew off to but a small distance. As night was coming on, the young hunter felt dismayed at the wildness and darkness of the place, and the strange company he had fallen in with; so he quietly withdrew, and returned empty handed to the camp, where, having told his story, he was heartily bantered by his more experienced comrades.

In the course of the evening, old Ryan came straggling into the camp, followed by his disciple, and as usual was received with hearty gratulations. He had lost himself yesterday, when hunting, and camped out all night, but had found our trail in the morning, and followed it up. He had passed some time at the beaver-dam, admiring the skill and solidity with which it had been constructed. "These beavers," said he, "are industrious little fellows. They are the knowingest varmint as I know; and I warrant the pond was stocked with them."

"Aye," said the Captain, "I have no doubt most of the small rivers we have passed are full of beaver. I would like to come and trap on these waters all winter."

"But would you not run the chance of being attacked by Indians?" asked one of the company.

"Oh, as to that, it would be safe enough here, in the winter time. There would be no Indians here until spring. I should want no more than two companions. Three persons are safer than a large number for trapping beaver. They can keep quiet, and need seldom fire a gun. A bear would serve them for food, for two months, taking care to turn every part of it to advantage."

A consultation was now held as to our future progress. We had thus far pursued a western course; and, having traversed the Cross Timber, were on the skirts of the Great Western Prairie.[2] We were still, however, in a very rough country, where food was scarce. The season was so far advanced that the grass was withered, and the prairies yielded no pasturage. The pea-vines of the bottoms, also, which had sustained our horses for some part of the journey, were nearly gone, and for several days past the poor animals had fallen off wofully both in flesh and spirit. The Indian fires on the prairies were approaching us from north, and south, and west; they might spread also from

[2] But they were *not* through the Cross Timbers. According to Ellsworth, "The prospect from the highest hills, showed us cross timbers still further west. We were assurd the praries lay but just beyond, and had been travelling with such anticipations for several days, and been dissappointed—Fearing we should not find the western extreemity without a very protracted journey I advised with my council (Mr Irving Capt Beans & Doct Holt) and we concluded to go south and strike the Canadian" (*Narrative*, 100).

the east, and leave a scorched desert between us and the frontier, in which our horses might be famished.

It was determined, therefore, to advance no further to the westward, but to shape our course more to the east, so as to strike the north fork of the Canadian, as soon as possible, where we hoped to find abundance of young cane; which, at this season of the year, affords the most nutritious pasturage for the horses; and, at the same time, attracts immense quantities of game. Here then we fixed the limits of our tour to the Far West, being within little more than a day's march to the boundary line of Texas.[3]

[3] A long day's march it would have been, for they were more than one hundred miles (by crow flight) from the Red River. On this day they were still north of the North Fork of the Canadian, which they would cross on October 25.

XXIV

Scarcity of Bread. Rencontre with Buffaloes.—Wild Turkeys.—Fall of a Buffalo Bull.

Th HE MORNING [October 24] broke bright and clear, but the camp had nothing of its usual gayety. The concert of the farm-yard was at an end; not a cock crew, nor dog barked; nor was there either singing or laughing; every one pursued his avocations quietly and gravely. The novelty of the expedition was wearing off. Some of the young men were getting as way-worn as their horses; and most of them, unaccustomed to the hunter's life, began to repine at its privations, What they most felt was the want of bread, their rations of flour having been exhausted for several days. The old hunters, who had often experienced this want, made light of it; and Beatte, accustomed when among the Indians to live for months without it, considered it a mere article of luxury. "Bread," he would say scornfully, "is only fit for a child."

About a quarter before eight o'clock, we turned our backs upon the Far West, and set off in a southeast course, along a gentle valley. After riding a few miles, Beatte, who kept parallel with us, along the ridge of a naked hill to our right, called out and made signals, as if something were coming round the hill to intercept us. Some who were near me cried out that it was a party of Pawnees. A skirt of thickets hid the approach of the supposed enemy from our view. We heard a trampling among the brushwood. My horse looked toward the place, snorted and pricked up his ears, when presently a couple of huge buffalo bulls, who had been alarmed by Beatte, came crashing through the brake, and making directly toward us. At sight of us they wheeled round, and scuttled along a narrow defile of the hill. In an instant half a score of rifles cracked off; there was a universal whoop and halloo, and away went half the troop, helter-skelter in pursuit, and myself among the number. The most of us soon pulled up, and gave over a chase which led through birch and brier, and break-neck ravines. Some few of the rangers persisted for a time; but eventually joined the line, slowly lagging one after another. One of them returned on foot; he had been thrown while in full chase; his rifle had been broken in the fall, and his horse, retaining the spirit of the rider, had kept on after the buffalo. It was a melancholy predicament to be reduced to; to be without horse or weapon in the midst of the Pawnee hunting grounds.

For my own part, I had been fortunate enough recently, by a further exchange, to get possession of the best horse in the troop; a full-blooded sorrel of excellent bottom, beautiful form, and most generous qualities.[1]

In such a situation, it almost seems as if a man changes his nature with his horse. I felt quite like another being, now that I had an animal under me, spirited yet gentle, docile to a remarkable degree, and easy, elastic, and rapid in all his movements. In a few days he became almost as much attached to me as a dog; would follow me when I dismounted, would come to me in the morning to be noticed and caressed; and would put his muzzle between me

[1] When Irving's bay sprained its shoulder on October 18, he shifted to a "jaded pony." The next day he traded this animal (with $70 "to boot" for Lieutenant George Caldwell's horse. Three or four days later he traded this horse, plus a $35 premium, for Private Clements' sorrel (Ellsworth, *Narrative*, 98–99). It must be remembered in this swapping that the horses belonged to the men, not to the government.

and my book, as I sat reading at the foot of a tree.[2] The feeling I had for this my dumb companion of the prairies, gave me some faint idea of that attachment the Arab is said to entertain for the horse that has borne him about the deserts.

After riding a few miles further, we came to a fine meadow with a broad clear stream winding through it, on the banks of which there was excellent pasturage. Here we at once came to a halt, in a beautiful grove of elms, on the site of an old Osage encampment. Scarcely had we dismounted, when a universal firing of rifles took place upon a large flock of turkeys, scattered about the grove, which proved to be a favorite roosting-place for these simple birds. They flew to the trees, and sat perched upon their branches, stretching out their long necks, and gazing in stupid astonishment, until eighteen of them were shot down.[3]

[2] What was Irving reading? Ellsworth told his wife of Irving's "joy at finding Pourteles had with him on our tour to the West, a French bible. He commenced it and read many pages but made a great merriment about the curious things that took place in those ancient days" (*Narrative*, 72). The only other book in the party, according to the Commissioner, was his own pocket testament (*ibid.*, 52).

[3] While in the Cross Timbers, Latrobe wrote, they generally sought "for a resting place in one of those spots of verdure in the vallies, where the fading green and yellow foliage of the cotton-wood poplar formed a pleasing contrast to the leafless oak, and held out promise of our obtaining the indespensable necessaries of wood and water. . . .

"Besides the above-mentioned poplar, together with hickory, walnut and willows, and the black and honey-locust, we found a rich under-growth of dogwood, persimmon, haws, vines with sweet and sour grapes—Chickasaw plums of various colours—sassafras, and abundance of green-briar or tear-blanket as it is familiarly called—besides sumac, the delight of the bear at this season.

"Such a Camp we occupied on the evening of the 24th, and a beau-

In the height of the carnage, word was brought that there were four buffaloes in a neighboring meadow. The turkeys were now abandoned for nobler game. The tired horses were again mounted, and urged to the chase. In a little while we came in sight of the buffaloes, looking like brown hillocks among the long green herbage. Beatte endeavored to get ahead of them and turn them towards us, that the inexperienced hunters might have a chance. They ran round the base of a rocky hill, that hid us from the sight. Some of us endeavored to cut across the hill, but became entrapped in a thick wood, matted with grapevines. My horse, who, under his former rider, had hunted the buffalo, seemed as much excited as myself, and endeavored to force his way through the bushes. At length we extricated ourselves, and galloping over the hill, I found our little Frenchman, Tonish, curvetting on horseback round a great buffalo which he had wounded too severely to fly, and which he was keeping employed until we should come up. There was a mixture of the grand and the comic, in beholding this tremendous animal and his fantastic assailant. The buffalo stood with his shaggy front always presented to his foe; his mouth open, his tongue parched, his eyes like coals of fire, and his tail erect with rage; every now and then he would make a faint rush upon his foe, who easily evaded his attack, capering and cutting all kinds of antics before him.[4]

_____

tiful one it was: we killed in its neighbourhood four Buffalo bulls and twenty turkeys, a piece of good fortune which we knew how to profit by, and, lighting our fires among the skeleton bowers remaining from a large Osage Camp of the preceding year, we here spent a contented night . . ." (*Rambler*, I, 213–14).

[4] Although he did not date it, perhaps it was this occasion that Latrobe had in mind when he wrote: "It was amusing to see the effect of the life we were leading, and the company we were associated with, on the spirits of the most peacable amongst us. There

We now made repeated shots at the buffalo, but they glanced into his mountain of flesh without proving mortal. He made a slow and grand retreat into the shallow river, turning upon his assailants whenever they pressed upon him; and when in the water, took his stand there as if prepared to sustain a siege. A rifle ball, however, more fatally lodged, sent a tremor through his frame. He turned and attempted to wade across the stream, but after tottering a few paces, slowly fell upon his side and expired. It was the fall of a hero, and we felt somewhat ashamed of the butchery that had effected it; but, after the first shot or two, we had reconciled it to our feelings, by the old plea of putting the poor animal out of his misery.

Two more buffaloes were killed this evening, but they were all bulls, the flesh of which is meagre and hard, at this season of the year. A fat buck yielded us more savory meat for our evening's repast.

was the good, kind-hearted Commissioner, whose career had never been stained up to the present time by act of violence to beast or bird, girding himself in his own quiet way for the expected rencontre with biped or quadruped savages, and breathing destruction to the innocent skunks and turkeys. There too was to be seen our friend Irving,—the kindly impulse of whose nature is to love every living thing,—ramming a couple of bullets home into a brace of old brass-barrelled pistols which had been furnished him from the armory at Fort Gibson, with a flourish of the ramrod, a compression of the lip, and a twinkle of the eye, which decidedly betokened mischief" (*Rambler*, I, 105 106). In this hunt of the 24th, Irving had a livelier share than he reported in the *Tour*: "Mr Irving found his pistols too small to be effectual, as he could not get near enough to the animal, with his horse He took Pourtcles gun (double barrell) and shot two balls with that, which took effect" (Ellsworth, *Narrative*, 105).

XXV

Ringing the Wild Horse.

WE LEFT the buffalo camp about eight o'clock [October 25],[1] and had a toilsome and harassing march of two hours, over ridges of hills, covered with a ragged meagre forest of scrub-oaks, and broken by deep gullies. Among the oaks I observed many of the most diminutive size; some not above a foot high, yet bearing abundance of small acorns. The whole of the Cross Timber, in fact, abounds, with mast. There is a pine-oak which produces an acorn pleasant to the taste, and ripening early in the season.

About ten o'clock in the morning, we came to where this line of rugged hills swept down into a valley, through which flowed the north fork of the Red River.[2] A beautiful meadow about half a mile wide, enamelled with yellow autumnal flowers, stretched for two or three miles along the foot of the hills, bordered on the opposite side by the river, whose banks were fringed with cotton-wood trees, the bright foliage of which refreshed and delighted the eye, after being wearied by the contemplation of monotonous wastes of brown forest.

The meadow was finely diversified by groves and clumps of trees, so happily dispersed, that they seemed as if set out by the hand of art. As we cast our eyes over

[1] On this morning Irving had for breakfast fritters fried in skunk fat as well as skunk stew: he "indulged his appetite *freely*—From this time no objections were made, against Pole Cats and they were a frequent dish" (Ellsworth, *Narrative,* 109).
[2] I.e., the North Fork of the Canadian.

this fresh and delightful valley, we beheld a troop of wild horses, quietly grazing on a green lawn, about a mile distant to our right, while to our left, at nearly the same distance, were several buffaloes; some feeding, others reposing and ruminating among the high rich herbage, under the shade of a clump of cotton-wood trees. The whole had the appearance of a broad beautiful tract of pasture land, on the highly ornamented estate of some gentleman farmer, with his cattle grazing about the lawns and meadows.

A council of war was now held, and it was determined to profit by the present favorable opportunity, and try our hand at the grand hunting manoeuvre, which is called ringing the wild horse. This requires a large party of horsemen, well mounted. They extend themselves in each direction, singly, at certain distances apart, and gradually form a ring of two or three miles in circumference, so as to surround the game. This has to be done with extreme care, for the wild horse is the most readily-alarmed inhabitant of the prairie, and can scent a hunter at a great distance, if to windward.

The ring being formed, two or three ride toward the horses, who start off in an opposite direction. Whenever they approach the bounds of the ring, however, a huntsman presents himself and turns them from their course. In this way they are checked and driven back at every point; and kept galloping round and round this magic circle, until, being completely tired down, it is easy for the hunters to ride up beside them, and throw the lariat over their heads. The prime horses of most speed, courage, and bottom, however, are apt to break through and escape, so that, in general, it is the second-rate horses that are taken.

Preparations were now made for a hunt of the kind. The pack horses were taken into the woods and firmly tied to trees, lest, in a rush of the wild horses, they should break away with them. Twenty-five men were then sent under the command of a lieutenant, to steal along the edge of the valley within the strip of wood that skirted the hills. They were to station themselves about fifty yards apart, within the edge of the woods, and not advance or show themselves until the horses dashed in that direction. Twenty-five men were sent across the valley, to steal in like manner along the river bank that bordered the opposite side, and to station themselves among the trees. A third party, of about the same number, was to form a line, stretching across the lower part of the valley, so as to connect the two wings. Beatte and our other half-breed, Antoine, together with the ever-officious Tonish, were to make a circuit through the woods so as to get to the upper part of the valley, in the rear of the horses and to drive them forward into the kind of sack that we had formed, while the two wings should join behind them and make a complete circle.

The flanking parties were quietly extending themselves, out of sight, on each side of the valley, and the residue were stretching themselves, like the links of a chain, across it, when the wild horses gave signs that they scented an enemy; snuffing the air, snorting, and looking about. At length they pranced off slowly toward the river, and disappeared behind a green bank. Here, had the regulations of the chase been observed, they would have been quietly checked and turned back by the advance of a hunter from among the trees; unluckily, however, we had our wild-fire Jack-o'-lantern little Frenchman to deal with. Instead of keeping quietly up the right side of the valley, to get above the horses, the moment he saw them move toward the river, he broke out of the covert of woods, and dashed furiously across the plain in pursuit of them, being mounted on one of the led horses belonging to the Count. This put an end to all system. The half-breeds and half a score of rangers joined in the chase. Away they all went over the green bank; in a moment or two the wild horses reappeared, and came thundering down the valley, with Frenchman, half-breeds, and rangers galloping and yelling like devils behind them. It was in vain that the line drawn across the valley attempted to check and turn back the fugitives. They were too hotly pressed by their pursuers; in their panic they dashed through the line, and clattered down the plain. The whole troop joined in the headlong chase, some of the rangers without hats or caps, their hair flying about their ears, others with handkerchiefs tied round their heads. The buffaloes, who had been calmly ruminating among the herbage, heaved up their huge forms, gazed for a moment with astonishment at the tempest that came scouring down the meadow, then turned and took a heavy-rolling flight. They were soon overtaken: the promiscuous throng were pressed together by the contracting sides of the valley, and away they went, pell-mell, hurry-scurry, wild buffalo, wild horse, wild huntsman, with clang and clatter, and whoop and halloo, that made the forests ring.

At length the buffaloes turned into a green brake on the river bank, while the horses dashed up a narrow defile of the hills, with their pursuers close at their heels. Beatte passed several of them, having fixed his eye upon a fine Pawnee horse, that had his ears slit, and saddle-marks upon his back. He pressed him gallantly, but lost him in the woods. Among the wild horses was a fine black mare, far gone with foal. In scrambling up the defile, she tripped and fell. A young ranger sprang from his horse, and seized her by the mane and muzzle. Another ranger dismounted, and came to his assistance. The mare struggled fiercely, kicking and biting, and striking with her fore feet, but a noose was slipped over her head, and her struggles were in vain. It was some time, however, before she gave over rearing and plunging, and lashing out with her feet on every side. The two rangers then led her along the valley by two long lariats, which enabled them to keep at a sufficient distance on each side to be out of the reach of her hoofs, and whenever she struck out in one direction, she was jerked in the other. In this way her spirit was gradually subdued.

As to little Scaramouch Tonish, who had marred the whole scene by his precipitancy,[3] he had been more successful than he deserved, having managed to catch a beautiful cream-colored colt, about seven months old, that had not strength to keep up with its companions. The mercurial little Frenchman was beside himself with exultation. It was amusing to see him with his prize. The colt would rear and kick, and struggle to get free, when Tonish would take him about the neck, wrestle with him, jump on his back, and cut as many antics as a monkey with a kitten. Nothing surprised me more, however, than to witness how soon these poor animals, thus taken from the unbounded freedom of the prairie, yielded to the dominion of man. In the course of two or three days the mare and colt went with the led horses, and became quite docile.[4]

[3] There is nothing in Ellsworth's account nor in Latrobe's to justify this comment about Tonish. It is an example either of Irving's prejudice against the Frenchman or of his determination to make a consistent literary characterization. Ellsworth has a particularly vivid account of this whole episode, *Narrative*, 109–11.

[4] It is to be regretted once more that Irving's notebook for this portion of his travels is lost: "Several pages of Mr Irvings book is filled with the incidents of these 2½ hours—Mr Irving did not join in the chase,—but rode from place to place, with his pistols girt about him, like a general, surveying the battle field after the fight is over" (Ellsworth, *Narrative*, 111).

⇜§ XXVI §⇝

Fording of the North Fork.—Dreary Scenery of the Cross Timber.—Scamper of Horses in the Night.—Osage War Party.—Effects of a Peace Harangue.—Buffalo.—Wild Horse.

ESUMING our march, we forded the North Fork, a rapid stream, and of a purity seldom to be found in the rivers of the prairies. It evidently had its source in high land, well supplied with springs After crossing the river,[1] we again ascended among hills, from one of which we had an extensive view over this belt of cross timber, and a cheerless prospect it was; hill beyond hill, forest beyond forest, all of one sad russet hue—excepting that here and there a line of green cotton-wood trees, sycamores, and willows, marked the course of some streamlet through a valley. A procession of buffaloes, moving slowly up the profile of one of those distant hills, formed a characteristic object in the savage scene. To the left, the eye stretched beyond this rugged wilderness of hills, and ravines, and ragged forests, to a prairie about ten miles off, extending in a clear blue line along the horizon. It was like looking from among rocks and breakers upon a distant tract of tranquil ocean. Unluckily, our route did not lie in that direction, we still had to traverse many a weary mile of the "Cross Timber."

We encamped toward evening in a valley, beside a scanty pool, under a scattered grove of elms, the upper branches of which were fringed with tufts of the mystic mistletoe. In the course of the night, the wild colt whinnied repeatedly; and about two hours before day, there was a sudden

[1] At about noon (Ellsworth, *Narrative,* 112). That morning they passed within a few miles east of the site of Oklahoma City.

stampede, or rush of horses, along the purlieus of the camp, with a snorting and neighing, and clattering of hoofs, that startled most of the rangers from their sleep, who listened in silence, until the sound died away like the rushing of a blast. As usual, the noise was at first attributed to some party of marauding Indians, but as the day dawned, a couple of wild horses were seen in a neighboring meadow, which scoured off on being approached. It was now supposed that a gang of them had dashed through our camp in the night. A general mustering of our horses took place, many were found scattered to a considerable distance, and several were not to be found. The prints of their hoofs, however, appeared deeply dinted in the soil, leading off at full speed into the waste, and their owners, putting themselves on the trail, set off in a weary search of them.

We had a ruddy daybreak [October 26], but the morning gathered up gray and lowering, with indications of an autumnal storm. We resumed our march silently and seriously, through a rough and cheerless country, from the highest points of which we could descry large prairies, stretching indefinitely westward. After travelling for two or three hours, as we were traversing a withered prairie, resembling a great brown heath, we beheld seven Osage warriors approaching at a distance. The sight of any human being in this lonely wilderness was interesting; it was like speaking a ship at sea. One of the Indians took the lead of his companions, and advanced toward us with head erect, chest thrown forward, and a free and noble mien. He was a fine-looking fellow, dressed in scarlet frock and fringed leggings of deer skin. His head was decorated with a white tuft, and he stepped forward with something of a martial air, swaying his bow and arrows in one hand.

We held some conversation with him through our interpreter, Beatte, and found that he and his companions had been with the main part of their tribe hunting the buffalo, and had met with great success; and he informed us, that in the course of another day's march, we would reach the prairies on the banks of the Grand Canadian, and find plenty of game. He added, that as their hunt was over, and the hunters on their return homeward, he and his comrades had set out on a war party, to waylay and hover about some Pawnee camp, in hopes of carrying off scalps or horses.

By this time his companions, who at first stood aloof, joined him. Three of them had indifferent fowling-pieces; the rest were armed with bows and arrows. I could not but admire the finely shaped heads and busts of these savages, and their graceful attitude and expressive gestures, as they stood conversing with our interpreter, and surrounded by a cavalcade of rangers. We endeavored to get one of them to join us, as we were desirous of seeing him hunt the buffalo with his bow and arrow. He seemed at first inclined to do so, but was dissuaded by his companions.

The worthy Commissioner now remembered his mission as pacificator, and made a speech, exhorting them to abstain from all offensive acts against the Pawnees; informing them of the plan of their father at Washington, to put an end to all war among his red children; and assuring them that he was sent to the frontier to establish a universal peace. He told them, therefore, to return quietly to their homes, with the certainty that the Pawnees would no longer molest them, but would soon regard them as brothers.

The Indians listened to the speech with their customary silence and decorum; after which, exchanging a few words among themselves, they bade us farewell, and pursued their way across the prairie.

Fancying that I saw a lurking smile in the countenance of our interpreter, Beatte, I privately inquired what the Indians had said to each other after hearing the speech. The leader, he said, had observed to his companions, that, as their great father intended so soon to put an end to all warfare, it behooved them to make the most of the little time that was left them. So they had departed, with re-doubled zeal, to pursue their project of horse stealing![2]

We had not long parted from the Indians before we discovered three buffaloes among the thickets of a marshy valley to our left. I set off with the Captain and several rangers, in pursuit of them. Stealing through a straggling grove, the Captain, who took the lead, got within rifle-shot, and wounded one of them in the flank. They all three made off in headlong panic, through thickets and brush-wood, and swamp and mire, bearing down every obstacle by their immense weight. The Captain and rangers soon gave up a chase which threatened to knock up their horses; I had got upon the traces of the wounded bull, however, and was in hopes of getting near enough to use my pistols, the only weapons with which I was provided; but before I could effect it, he reached the foot of a rocky hill, covered with post-oak and brambles, and plunged forward, dashing and crashing along, with neck or nothing fury, where it would have been madness to have followed him.

The chase had led me so far on one side, that it was some time before I regained the trail of our troop. As I was slowly ascending a hill, a fine black mare came prancing

[2] In his own journal Ellsworth wrote: "Mr Irving has added a little here [in his notebook] to make a good story, and says the Osages listened with attention to what I said, but remarked 'they go and steal some horses before peace was made as they must not steal any afterwards'—but this is certainly by way of addenda" (*Narrative*, 114).

round the summit, and was close to me before she was aware. At sight of me she started back, then turning, swept at full speed down into the valley, and up the opposite hill, with flowing mane and tail, and action free as air. I gazed after her as long as she was in sight, and breathed a wish that so glorious an animal might never come under the degrading thraldom of whip and curb, but remain a free rover of the prairies.

XXVII

*Foul Weather Encampment.—Anecdotes of Bear Hunting.
—Indian Notions about Omens.—Scruples Respecting the
Dead.*

O N OVERTAKING the troop, I found it encamping in a
rich bottom of woodland, traversed by a small stream,
running between deep crumbling banks.[1] A sharp cracking off of rifles was kept up for some time in various directions, upon a numerous flock of turkeys, scampering among
the thickets, or perched upon the trees. We had not been
long at a halt, when a drizzling rain ushered in the autumnal storm that had been brewing. Preparations were immediately made to weather it; our tent was pitched, and our
saddles, saddle-bags, packages of coffee, sugar, salt, and
every thing else that could be damaged by the rain, were
gathered under its shelter. Our men, Beatte, Tonish, and
Antoine, drove stakes with forked ends into the ground,
laid poles across them for rafters, and thus made a shed or
penthouse, covered with bark and skins, sloping toward
the wind, and open toward the fire. The rangers formed
similar shelters of bark and skins, or of blankets stretched
on poles, supported by forked stakes, with great fires in
front.[2]

These precautions were well timed. The rain set in sul-
lenly and steadily, and kept on, with slight intermissions,
for two days. The brook which flowed peaceably on our

[1] Grand Bayou, a tributary of the Canadian, according to Latrobe
(*Rambler*, I, 216). More likely this stream flowed into Little River,
a branch of the Canadian.
[2] They remained in this camp through the twenty-eighth. It
could not have been far east of present-day Norman, Oklahoma.

arrival, swelled into a turbid and boiling torrent, and the forest became little better than a mere swamp. The men gathered under their shelters of skins and blankets, or sat cowering round their fires; while columns of smoke curling up among the trees, and diffusing themselves in the air, spread a blue haze through the woodland. Our poor, way-worn horses, reduced by weary travel and scanty pasturage, lost all remaining spirit, and stood, with drooping heads, flagging ears, and half closed eyes, dozing and steaming in the rain: while the yellow autumnal leaves, at every shaking of the breeze, came wavering down around them.[3]

Notwithstanding the bad weather, however, our hunters were not idle, but during the intervals of the rain, sallied forth on horseback to prowl through the woodland. Every now and then the sharp report of a distant rifle boded the death of a deer. Venison in abundance was brought in. Some busied themselves under the sheds, flaying and cutting up the carcasses, or round the fires with spits and camp-kettles, and a rude kind of feasting, or rather gormandizing, prevailed throughout the camp. The axe was continually at work, and wearied the forest with its echoes. Crash! some mighty tree would come down; in a few minutes its limbs would be blazing and crackling

[3] During this layover (on the twenty-seventh), Latrobe wrote: "As to the inhabitants of our tent — we lay watching the preparations for breakfast like so many cats. Pourtales was unwell, having indulged largely in the luxuries of persimmon, sloes, skunks, and sour grapes, and refused both medicine and comfort. In the intervals of conversation the Commissioner sat the very image of patience, and gave himself up to speculation. Mr. Irving dozed by fits and starts, or perused the only volume of which our camp library was composed; and between whiles, peeped out from the folds of the tent upon the groups around, scanning the individuals composing them with his own good-natured and humoursome eye" (*Rambler*, I, 219).

on the huge camp-fires, with some luckless deer roasting before it, that had once sported beneath its shade.

The change of weather had taken sharp hold of our little Frenchman. His meagre frame, composed of bones and whipcord, was racked with rheumatic pains and twinges. He had the toothache—the earache—his face was tied up— he had shooting pains in every limb: yet all seemed but to increase his restless activity, and he was in an incessant fidget about the fire, roasting, and stewing, and groaning, and scolding, and swearing.

Our man Beatte returned grim and mortified, from hunting. He had come upon a bear of formidable dimensions, and wounded him with a rifle-shot. The bear took to the brook, which was swollen and rapid. Beatte dashed in after him and assailed him in the rear with his hunting-knife. At every blow the bear turned furiously upon him, with a terrific display of white teeth. Beatte, having a foothold in the brook, was enabled to push him off with his rifle, and, when he turned to swim, would flounder after, and attempt to hamstring him. The bear, however, succeeded in scrambling off among the thickets, and Beatte had to give up the chase.

This adventure, if it produced no game, brought up at least several anecdotes, round the evening fire, relative to bear hunting, in which the grizzly bear figured conspicuously. This powerful and ferocious animal is a favorite theme of hunters' story, both among red and white men; and his enormous claws are worn round the neck of an Indian brave, as a trophy more honorable than a human scalp. He is now scarcely seen below the upper prairies, and the skirts of the Rocky Mountains. Other bears are formidable when wounded and provoked, but seldom make battle when allowed to escape. The grizzly bear, alone, of all the animals of our Western wilds, is prone to unpro-

voked hostility. His prodigious size and strength make
him a formidable opponent; and his great tenacity of life
often baffles the skill of the hunter, notwithstanding repeated shots of the rifle, and wounds of the hunting-knife.

One of the anecdotes related on this occasion, gave a
picture of the accidents and hard shifts to which our frontier rovers are inured. A hunter, while in pursuit of a deer,
fell into one of those deep funnel-shaped pits, formed on
the prairies by the settling of the waters after heavy rains,
and known by the name of sink-holes. To his great hor-
ror, he came in contact, at the bottom, with a huge grizzly
bear. The monster grappled him; a deadly contest ensued,
in which the poor hunter was severely torn and bitten,
and had a leg and an arm broken, but succeeded in killing
his rugged foe. For several days he remained at the bottom
of the pit, too much crippled to move, and subsisting on
the raw flesh of the bear, during which time he kept his
wounds open, that they might heal gradually and effec-
tually. He was at length enabled to scramble to the top
of the pit, and so out upon the open prairie. With great
difficulty he crawled to a ravine, formed by a stream, then
nearly dry. Here he took a delicious draught of water,
which infused new life into him; then dragging himself
along from pool to pool, he supported himself by small
fish and frogs.

One day he saw a wolf hunt down and kill a deer in
the neighboring prairie. He immediately crawled forth
from the ravine, drove off the wolf, and, lying down beside the carcass of the deer, remained there until he made
several hearty meals, by which his strength was much re-
cruited.

Returning to the ravine, he pursued the course of the
brook, until it grew to be a considerable stream. Down
this he floated, until he came to where it emptied into the

Mississippi [*sic*]. Just at the mouth of the stream, he found a forked tree, which he launched with some difficulty, and, getting astride of it, committed himself to the current of the mighty river. In this way he floated along, until he arrived opposite the fort at Council Bluffs. Fortunately he arrived there in the daytime, otherwise he might have floated, unnoticed, past this solitary post, and perished in the idle waste of waters. Being descried from the fort, a canoe was sent to his relief, and he was brought to shore more dead than alive, where he soon recovered from his wounds, but remained maimed for life.[4]

Our man Beatte had come out of his contest with the bear very much worsted and discomfited. His drenching in the brook, together with the recent change of weather, had brought on rheumatic pains in his limbs, to which he is subject. Though ordinarily a fellow of undaunted spirit, and above all hardship, yet he now sat down by the fire, gloomy and dejected, and for once gave way to repining. Though in the prime of life, and of a robust frame, and apparently iron constitution, yet, by his own account, he was little better than a mere wreck. He was, in fact, a living monument of the hardships of wild frontier life. Baring his left arm, he showed it warped and contracted by a former attack of rheumatism; a malady with which the Indians are often afflicted; for their exposure to the vicissitudes of the elements does not produce that perfect hardihood and insensibility to the changes of the seasons that

[4] Under date of October 18, Ellsworth told this story better and in more detail; he credited it to Captain Bean, who "knows the characters concerned personally"—they had been members of Ashley's band of hunters (*Narrative*, 53–57). According to Henry L. Wagner and Charles L. Camp, the earliest version of the Hugh Glass story was published in the Philadelphia *Port Folio*, March, 1825 (*The Plains and the Rockies* [Columbus, Ohio, Long's College Book Company, 1953], 52–54).

many are apt to imagine. He bore the scars of various maims and bruises; some received in hunting, some in Indian warfare. His right arm had been broken by a fall from his horse; at another time his steed had fallen with him, and crushed his left leg.

"I am all broke to pieces and good for nothing," said he; "I no care now what happen to me any more." "However," added he, after a moment's pause, "for all that, it would take a pretty strong man to put me down, anyhow."

I drew from him various particulars concerning himself, which served to raise him in my estimation. His residence was on the Neosho, in an Osage hamlet or neighborhood, under the superintendence of a worthy missionary from the banks of the Hudson, by the name of Requa, who was endeavoring to instruct these savages in the art of agriculture, and to make husbandmen and herdsmen of them. I had visited this agricultural mission of Requa in the course of my recent tour along the frontier, and had considered it more likely to produce solid advantages to the poor Indians, than any of the mere praying and preaching missions along the border.[5]

In this neighborhood, Pierre Beatte had his little farm, his Indian wife, and his half-breed children; and aided Mr. Requa in his endeavors to civilize the habits, and meliorate the condition of the Osage tribe. Beatte had been brought

---

[5] William R. Requa (1795–1886), born in Westchester County, New York, had come out to Union Mission in 1821. In 1830, he moved Hopefield Mission from a location within four miles of Union Mission to a spot twenty-five miles north of Union, on the west bank of the Neosho just below Cabin or Plank Cabin Creek. There Irving and his fellow travelers had noon dinner on October 6 (*Western Journals*, 107–108). In 1832, twenty-two Indian families were resident in the village. Requa mentioned the visit of this party in a letter written to the American Board of Commissioners of Foreign Missions on November 27, 1832.

up a Catholic, and was inflexible in his religious faith; he could not pray with Mr. Requa, he said, but he could work with him, and he evinced a zeal for the good of his savage relations and neighbors. Indeed, though his father had been French, and he himself had been brought up in communion with the whites, he evidently was more of an Indian in his tastes, and his heart yearned toward his mother's nation. When he talked to me of the wrongs and insults that the poor Indians suffered in their intercourse with the rough settlers on the frontiers: when he described the precarious and degraded state of the Osage tribe, diminished in numbers, broken in spirit, and almost living on sufferance in the land where they once figured so heroically, I could see his veins swell, and his nostrils distend with indignation; but he would check the feeling with a strong exertion of Indian self-command, and, in a manner, drive it back into his bosom.

He did not hesitate to relate an instance wherein he had joined his kindred Osages, in pursuing and avenging themselves on a party of white men who had committed a flagrant outrage upon them; and I found, in the encounter that took place, Beatte had shown himself the complete Indian.

He had more than once accompanied his Osage relations in their wars with the Pawnees, and related a skirmish which took place on the borders of these very hunting grounds, in which several Pawnees were killed. We should pass near the place, he said, in the course of our tour, and the unburied bones and skulls of the slain were still to be seen there. The surgeon of the troop, who was present at our conversation, pricked up his ears at this intelligence. He was something of a phrenologist, and offered Beatte a handsome reward if he would procure him one of the skulls.

Beatte regarded him for a moment with a look of stern surprise.

"No!" said he at length, "dat too bad! I have heart strong enough—I no care kill, but *let the dead alone!*"

He added, that once in travelling with a party of white men, he had slept in the same tent with a doctor, and found that he had a Pawnee skull among his baggage: he at once renounced the doctor's tent, and his fellowship. "He try to coax me," said Beatte, "but I say no, we must part—I no keep such company."

In the temporary depression of his spirits, Beatte gave way to those superstitious forebodings to which Indians are prone. He had sat for some time, with his cheek upon his hand, gazing into the fire. I found his thoughts were wandering back to his humble home, on the banks of the Neosho; he was sure, he said, that he should find some one of his family ill, or dead, on his return: his left eye had twitched and twinkled for two days past; an omen which always boded some misfortune of the kind.

Such are the trivial circumstances which, when magnified into omens, will shake the souls of these men of iron. The least sign of mystic and sinister portent is sufficient to turn a hunter or a warrior from his course, or to fill his mind with apprehensions of impending evil. It is this superstitious propensity, common to the solitary and savage lovers of the wilderness, that gives such powerful influence to the prophet and the dreamer.

The Osages, with whom Beatte had passed much of his life, retain these superstitious fancies and rites in much of their original force. They all believe in the existence of the soul after its separation from the body, and that it carries with it all its mortal tastes and habitudes. At an Osage village in the neighborhood of Beatte, one of the chief warriors lost an only child, a beautiful girl, of a very tender age. All her playthings were buried with her. Her favorite little horse, also, was killed, and laid in the grave beside her, that she might have it to ride in the land of spirits.[6]

I will here add a little story, which I picked up in the course of my tour through Beatte's country, and which illustrates the superstitions of his Osage kindred. A large party of Osages had been encamped for some time on the borders of a fine stream, called the Nickanansa. Among them was a young hunter, one of the bravest and most graceful of the tribe, who was to be married to an Osage girl, who, for her beauty, was called the Flower of the Prairies. The young hunter left her for a time among her relatives in the encampment, and went to St. Louis, to dispose of the products of his hunting, and purchase ornaments for his bride. After an absence of some weeks, he returned to the banks of the Nickanansa, but the camp was no longer there; and the bare frames of the lodges and the brands of extinguished fires alone marked its place. At a distance he beheld a female seated, as if weeping, by the side of the stream. It was his affianced bride. He ran to embrace her, but she turned mournfully away. He dreaded lest some evil had befallen the camp.

"Where are our people?" cried he.

"They are gone to the banks of the Wagrushka."

"And what art thou doing here alone?"

"Waiting for thee."

"Then let us hasten to join our people on the banks of the Wagrushka."

He gave her his pack to carry, and walked ahead, according to the Indian custom.

They came to where the smoke of the distant camp was

[6] This story is from a notation made on October 4; apparently Irving had it from A. P. Chouteau (*Western Journals*, 101).

seen rising from the woody margin of the stream. The girl seated herself at the foot of a tree. "It is not proper for us to return together," said she; "I will wait here."

The young hunter proceeded to the camp alone, and was received by his relations with gloomy countenances.

"What evil has happened," said he, "that ye are all so sad?"

No one replied.

He turned to his favorite sister, and bade her go forth, seek his bride, and conduct her to the camp.

"Alas!" cried she, "how shall I seek her? She died a few days since."

The relations of the young girl now surrounded him, weeping and wailing; but he refused to believe the dismal tidings. "But a few moments since," cried he, "I left her alone and in health. come with me, and I will conduct you to her."

He led the way to the tree where she had seated herself, but she was no longer there, and his pack lay on the ground. The fatal truth struck him to the heart; he fell to the ground dead.

I give this simple little story almost in the words in which it was related to me, as I lay by the fire in an evening encampment on the banks of the haunted stream where it is said to have happened.[7]

[7] This story had been told by Colonel Chouteau on October 4 (*Western Journals*, 100–101). The stream was Labette Creek, which enters the Neosho River from the west near the Kansas-Oklahoma line.

XXVIII

A Secret Expedition.—Deer Bleating.—Magic Balls.

O<small>N</small> the following morning [October 28] we were rejoined by the rangers who had remained at the last encampment, to seek for the stray horses. They had tracked
them for a considerable distance through bush and brake,
and across streams, until they found them cropping the
herbage on the edge of a prairie. Their heads were in the
direction of the fort, and they were evidently grazing their
way homeward, heedless of the unbounded freedom of
the prairie so suddenly laid open to them.

About noon the weather held up, and I observed a mysterious consultation going on between our half-breeds and
Tonish; it ended in a request that we would dispense with
the services of the latter for a few hours, and permit him
to join his comrades in a grand foray. We objected that
Tonish was too much disabled by aches and pains for such
an undertaking; but he was wild with eagerness for the
mysterious enterprise, and, when permission was given
him, seemed to forget all his ailments in an instant.

In a short time the trio was equipped and on horseback;
with rifles on their shoulders and handkerchiefs twisted
round their heads, evidently bound for a grand scamper.
As they passed by the different lodges of the camp, the
vain-glorious little Frenchman could not help boasting to
the right and left of the great things he was about to
achieve; though the taciturn Beatte, who rode in advance,
would every now and then check his horse, and look back

at him with an air of stern rebuke. It was hard, however, to make the loquacious Tonish play "Indian."

Several of the hunters, likewise, sallied forth, and the prime old woodman, Ryan, came back early in the afternoon, with ample spoil, having killed a buck and two fat does. I drew near to a group of rangers that had gathered round him as he stood by the spoil, and found they were discussing the merits of a stratagem sometimes used in deer hunting. This consists in imitating, with a small instrument called a bleat, the cry of the fawn, so as to lure the doe within reach of the rifle. There are bleats of various kinds, suited to calm or windy weather, and to the age of the fawn. The poor animal, deluded by them, in its anxiety about its young, will sometimes advance close up to the hunter. "I once bleated a doe," said a young hunter, "until it came within twenty yards of me, and presented a sure mark. I levelled my rifle three times, but had not the heart to shoot, for the poor doe looked so wistfully, that it in a manner made my heart yearn. I thought of my own mother, and how anxious she used to be about me when I was a child; so to put an end to the matter, I gave a halloo, and started the doe out of rifle-shot in a moment."

"And you did right," cried honest old Ryan. "For my part, I never could bring myself to bleating deer. I've been with hunters who had bleats, and have made them throw them away. It is a rascally trick to take advantage of a mother's love for her young."

Toward evening, our three worthies returned from their mysterious foray. The tongue of Tonish gave notice of their approach long before they came in sight; for he was vociferating at the top of his lungs, and rousing the attention of the whole camp. The lagging gait and reeking flanks of their horses, gave evidence of hard rid-

ing; and, on nearer approach, we found them hung round
with meat like a butcher's shambles. In fact, they had been
scouring an immense prairie that extended beyond the
forest, and which was covered with herds of buffalo. Of
this prairie, and the animals upon it, Beatte had received
intelligence a few days before, in his conversation with the
Osages: but had kept the information a secret from the
rangers, that he and his comrades might have the first dash
at the game. They had contented themselves with killing
four; though, if Tonish might be believed, they might
have slain them by scores.[1]

These tidings, and the buffalo meat brought home in
evidence, spread exultation through the camp, and every
one looked forward with joy to a buffalo hunt on the
prairies. Tonish was again the oracle of the camp, and held
forth by the hour to a knot of listeners, crouched round
the fire, with their shoulders up to their ears. He was now
more boastful than ever of his skill as a marksman. All his
want of success in the early part of our march, he attributed
to being "out of luck," if not "spell-bound"; and finding
himself listened to with apparent credulity, gave an instance of the kind, which he declared had happened to
himself, but which was evidently a tale picked up among
his relations, the Osages.

According to this account, when about fourteen years
of age, as he was one day hunting, he saw a white deer
come out from a ravine. Crawling near to get a shot, he beheld another and another come forth, until there were
seven, all as white as snow. Having crept sufficiently near,
he singled one out and fired, but without effect; the deer
remained unfrightened. He loaded and fired again, and
again he missed. Thus he continued firing and missing until
all his ammunition was expended, and the deer remained

[1] Ellsworth said three (*Narrative*, 120).

without a wound. He returned home despairing of his skill as a marksman, but was consoled by an old Osage hunter. These white deer, said he, have a charmed life, and can only be killed by bullets of a particular kind.

The old Indian cast several balls for Tonish, but would not suffer him to be present on the occasion, nor inform him of the ingredients and mystic ceremonials.

Provided with these balls, Tonish again set out in quest of the white deer, and succeeded in finding them. He tried at first with ordinary balls, but missed as before. A magic ball, however, immediately brought a fine buck to the ground. Whereupon the rest of the herd immediately disappeared and were never seen again.[2]

(Oct. 29.). The morning opened gloomy and lowering; but toward eight o'clock the sun struggled forth and lighted up the forest, and the notes of the bugle gave signal to prepare for marching. Now began a scene of bustle, and clamor, and gayety. Some were scampering and brawling after their horses, some were riding in bare-backed, and driving in the horses of their comrades. Some were stripping the poles of the wet blankets that had served for shelters; others packing up with all possible dispatch, and loading the baggage horses as they arrived, while others were cracking off their damp rifles and charging them afresh, to be ready for the sport.

About ten o'clock, we began our march. I loitered in the rear of the troop as it forded the turbid brook and defiled through the labyrinths of the forest. I always felt disposed to linger until the last straggler disappeared among the trees and the distant note of the bugle died upon the ear, that I might behold the wilderness relapsing into si-

[2] This story Irving set down in the undated paragraphs at the end of his *next* notebook, October 31–November 10. There he gave Tonish's age as "about 15 years" (*Western Journals*, 152–53).

lence and solitude. In the present instance, the deserted scene of our late bustling encampment had a forlorn and desolate appearance. The surrounding forest had been in many places trampled into a quagmire. Trees felled and partly hewn in pieces, and scattered in huge fragments; tent-poles stripped of their covering; smouldering fires, with great morsels of roasted venison and buffalo meat, standing in wooden spits before them, hacked and slashed by the knives of hungry hunters; while around were strewed the hides, the horns, the antlers, and bones of buffaloes and deer, with uncooked joints, and unplucked turkeys, left behind with that reckless improvidence and wastefulness which young hunters are apt to indulge when in a neighborhood where game abounds. In the meantime a score or two of turkey-buzzards, or vultures, were already on the wing, wheeling their magnificent flight high in the air, and preparing for a descent upon the camp as soon as it should be abandoned.

The Grand Prairie.—A Buffalo Hunt.

Aᴿᴛᴇʀ proceeding about two hours in a southerly direction, we emerged toward mid-day from the dreary belt of the Cross Timber, and to our infinite delight beheld "the great Prairie" stretching to the right and left before us.[1] We could distinctly trace the meandering course of the main Canadian, and various smaller streams, by the strips of green forest that bordered them. The landscape was vast and beautiful. There is always an expansion of feeling in looking upon these boundless and fertile wastes; but I was doubly conscious of it after emerging from our "close dungeon of innumerable boughs."

From a rising ground Beatte pointed out the place where he and his comrades had killed the buffaloes; and we beheld several black objects moving in the distance, which he said were part of the herd. The Captain determined to shape his course to a woody bottom about a mile distant, and to encamp there for a day or two, by way of having a regular buffalo hunt, and getting a supply of provisions. As the troop defiled along the slope of the hill toward the camping ground, Beatte proposed to my messmates and myself, that we should put ourselves under his guidance, promising to take us where we should have plenty of sport.

[1] Latrobe (*Rambler,* I, 222) called this the Big Prairie; obviously its French name was Grand Prairie. Josiah Gregg's map (1844) shows it extending west along the north bank of the Canadian for fifty miles or more and perhaps thirty broad. Beyond it, on the right bank of the river, lay another belt of Cross Timbers.

Leaving the line of march, therefore, we diverged toward the prairie; traversing a small valley, and ascending a gentle swell of land. As we reached the summit, we beheld a gang of wild horses about a mile off. Beatte was immediately on the alert, and no longer thought of buffalo hunting. He was mounted on his powerful half-wild horse, with a lariat coiled at the saddle-bow, and set off in pursuit; while we remained on a rising ground watching his maneuvers with great solicitude. Taking advantage of a strip of woodland, he stole quietly along, so as to get close to them before he was perceived. The moment they caught sight of him a grand scamper took place. We watched him skirting along the horizon like a privateer in full chase of a merchantman; at length he passed over the brow of a ridge, and down into a shallow valley; in a few moments he was on the opposite hill, and close upon one of the horses. He was soon head and head, and appeared to be trying to noose his prey; but they both disappeared again below the hill, and we saw no more of them. It turned out afterward that he had noosed a powerful horse, but could not hold him, and had lost his lariat in the attempt.

While we were waiting for his return, we perceived two buffalo bulls descending a slope, toward a stream, which wound through a ravine fringed with trees. The young Count and myself endeavored to get near them under covert of the trees. They discovered us while we were yet three or four hundred yards off, and turning about, retreated up the rising ground. We urged our horses across the ravine, and gave chase. The immense weight of head and shoulders, causes the buffalo to labor heavily up hill; but it accelerates his descent. We had the advantage, therefore, and gained rapidly upon the fugitives, though it was difficult to get our horses to approach them, their very scent inspiring them with terror. The Count, who had a

double-barrelled gun loaded with ball, fired, but it missed.
The bulls now altered their course, and galloped down hill
with headlong rapidity. As they ran in different directions,
we each singled one and separated. I was provided with a
brace of veteran brass-barrelled pistols, which I had borrowed at Fort Gibson, and which had evidently seen some
service.[2] Pistols are very effective in buffalo hunting, as
the hunter can ride up close to the animal, and fire at it
while at full speed; whereas the long heavy rifles used on
the frontier, cannot be easily managed, nor discharged
with accurate aim from horseback. My object, therefore,
was to get within pistol shot of the buffalo. This was no
very easy matter. I was well mounted on a horse of excellent speed and bottom, that seemed eager for the chase,
and soon overtook the game; but the moment he came
nearly parallel, he would keep sheering off, with ears
forked and pricked forward, and every symptom of aver
sion and alarm. It was no wonder. Of all animals, a buffalo,
when close pressed by the hunter, has an aspect the most
diabolical. His two short black horns, curve out of a huge
frontlet of shaggy hair; his eyes glow like coals; his mouth
is open, his tongue parched and drawn up into a half cres-
cent; his tail is erect, and tufted and whisking about in
the air, he is a perfect picture of mingled rage and terror.

It was with difficulty I urged my horse sufficiently near,
when, taking aim, to my chagrin, both pistols missed fire.
Unfortunately the locks of these veteran weapons were so
much worn, that in the gallop, the priming had been shaken
out of the pans. At the snapping of the last pistol I was
close upon the buffalo, when, in his despair, he turned
round with a sudden snort and rushed upon me. My horse
wheeled about as if on a pivot, made a convulsive spring,

[2] These pistols have already been noticed in note 4, Chapter
XXIV.

and, as I had been leaning on one side with pistol extended, I came near being thrown at the feet of the buffalo.

Three or four bounds of the horse carried us out of the reach of the enemy; who, having merely turned in desperate self-defense, quickly resumed his flight. As soon as I could gather in my panic-stricken horse, and prime the pistols afresh, I again spurred in pursuit of the buffalo, who had slackened his speed to take breath. On my approach he again set off full tilt, heaving himself forward with a heavy rolling gallop, dashing with headlong precipitation through brakes and ravines, while several deer and wolves, startled from their coverts by his thundering career, ran helter-skelter to right and left across the waste.

A gallop across the prairies in pursuit of game is by no means so smooth a career as those may imagine, who have only the idea of an open level plain. It is true, the prairies of the hunting ground are not so much entangled with flowering plants and long herbage as the lower prairies, and are principally covered with short buffalo grass; but they are diversified by hill and dale, and where most level, are apt to be cut up by deep rifts and ravines, made by torrents after rains; and which, yawning from an even surface, are almost like pitfalls in the way of the hunter, checking him suddenly, when in full career, or subjecting him to the risk of limb and life. The plains, too, are beset by burrowing holes of small animals, in which the horse is apt to sink to the fetlock, and throw both himself and his rider. The late rain had covered some parts of the prairie, where the ground was hard, with a thin sheet of water, through which the horse had to splash his way. In other parts there were innumerable shallow hollows, eight or ten feet in diameter, made by the buffaloes, who wallow in sand and mud like swine. These being filled with water, shone like mirrors, so that the horse was continually leaping over them or springing on one side. We had reached, too, a rough part of the prairie, very much broken and cut up; the buffalo, who was running for his life, took no heed of his course, plunging down break-neck ravines, where it was necessary to skirt the borders in search of a safer descent. At length we came to where a winter stream had torn a deep chasm across the whole prairie, leaving open jagged rocks, and forming a long glen bordered by steep crumbling cliffs of mingled stone and clay. Down one of these the buffalo flung himself, half tumbling, half leaping, and then scuttled along the bottom; while I, seeing all further pursuit useless, pulled up, and gazed quietly after him from the border of the cliff, until he disappeared amidst the windings of the ravine.

Nothing now remained but to turn my steed and rejoin my companions. Here at first was some little difficulty. The ardor of the chase had betrayed me into a long, heedless gallop. I now found myself in the midst of a lonely waste, in which the prospect was bounded by undulating swells of land, naked and uniform, where, from the deficiency of landmarks and distinct features, an inexperienced man may become bewildered, and lose his way as readily as in the wastes of the ocean. The day, too, was overcast, so that I could not guide myself by the sun; my only mode was to retrace the track my horse had made in coming, though this I would often lose sight of, where the ground was covered with parched herbage.

To one unaccustomed to it, there is something inexpressibly lonely in the solitude of a prairie. The loneliness of a forest seems nothing to it. There the view is shut in by trees, and the imagination is left free to picture some livelier scene beyond. But here we have an immense extent of landscape without a sign of human existence. We have the consciousness of being far, far beyond the bounds of human habitation; we feel as if moving in the midst of a desert world. As my horse lagged slowly back over the scenes of our late scamper, and the delirium of the chase had passed away, I was peculiarly sensible to these circumstances. The silence of the waste was now and then broken by the cry of a distant flock of pelicans, stalking like spectres about a shallow pool; sometimes by the sinister croaking of a raven in the air, while occasionally a scoundrel wolf would scour off from before me; and, having attained a safe distance, would sit down and howl and whine with tones that gave a dreariness to the surrounding solitude.

After pursuing my way for some time, I descried a horseman on the edge of a distant hill, and soon recognized him to be the Count. He had been equally unsuccessful with myself; we were shortly after rejoined by our worthy comrade, the Virtuoso, who, with spectacles on nose, had made two or three ineffectual shots from horseback.

We determined not to seek the camp until we had made one more effort. Casting our eyes about the surrounding waste, we descried a herd of buffalo about two miles distant, scattered apart, and quietly grazing near a small strip of trees and bushes. It required but little stretch of fancy to picture them so many cattle grazing on the edge of a common, and that the grove might shelter some lowly farm-house.

We now formed our plan to circumvent the herd, and by getting on the other side of them, to hunt them in the direction where we knew our camp to be situated: otherwise, the pursuit might take us to such a distance as to render it impossible to find our way back before nightfall. Taking a wide circuit, therefore, we moved slowly and cautiously, pausing occasionally, when we saw any of the herd desist from grazing. The wind fortunately set from them, otherwise they might have scented us and have taken the alarm. In this way, we succeeded in getting round the herd without disturbing it. It consisted of about forty head, bulls, cows, and calves. Separating to some distance from each other, we now approached slowly in a parallel line, hoping by degrees to steal near without exciting attention. They began, however, to move off quietly, stopping at every step or two to graze, when suddenly a bull that, unobserved by us, had been taking his siesta under a clump of trees to our left, roused himself from his lair, and hastened to join his companions. We were still at a considerable distance, but the game had taken the alarm. We quickened our pace, they broke into a gallop, and now commenced a full chase.

As the ground was level, they shouldered along with great speed, following each other in a line; two or three bulls bringing up the rear, the last of whom, from his enormous size and venerable frontlet, and beard of sunburnt hair, looked like the patriarch of the herd; and as if he might long have reigned the monarch of the prairie.

There is a mixture of the awful and the comic in the look of these huge animals, as they bear their great bulk forward, with an up and down motion of the unwieldy head and shoulders; their tail cocked up like the queue of Pantaloon in a pantomime, the end whisking about in a fierce yet whimsical style, and their eyes glaring venomously with an expression of fright and fury.

For some time I kept parallel with the line, without being able to force my horse within pistol shot, so much had he been alarmed by the assault of the buffalo in the preceding chase. At length I succeeded, but was again balked by my pistols missing fire. My companions, whose horses were less fleet, and more way-worn, could not overtake the herd; at length Mr. L., who was in the rear of the line, and losing ground, levelled his double-barrelled gun, and fired a long raking shot. It struck a buffalo just above the loins, broke its back-bone, and brought it to the ground. He stopped and alighted to dispatch his prey, when borrowing his gun, which had yet a charge remaining in it, I put my horse to his speed, again overtook the herd which was thundering along, pursued by the Count. With my present weapon there was no need of urging my horse to such close quarters; galloping along parallel, therefore, I singled out a buffalo, and by a fortunate shot brought it down on the spot. The ball had struck a vital part; it could not move from the place where it fell, but lay there struggling in mortal agony, while the rest of the herd kept on their headlong career across the prairie.

Dismounting, I now fettered my horse to prevent his straying, and advanced to contemplate my victim. I am nothing of a sportsman; I had been prompted to this unwonted exploit by the magnitude of the game, and the excitement of an adventurous chase. Now that the excitement was over, I could not but look with commiseration upon the poor animal that lay struggling and bleeding at my feet. His very size and importance, which had before inspired me with eagerness, now increased my compunction. It seemed as if I had inflicted pain in proportion to the bulk of my victim, and as if there were a hundred-fold greater waste of life than there would have been in the destruction of an animal of inferior size.

To add to these after-qualms of conscience, the poor animal lingered in his agony. He had evidently received a mortal wound, but death might be long in coming. It would not do to leave him here to be torn piecemeal, while yet alive, by the wolves that had already snuffed his blood, and were skulking and howling at a distance, and waiting for my departure; and by the ravens that were flapping about, croaking dismally in the air. It became now an act of mercy to give him his quietus, and put him out of his misery. I primed one of the pistols, therefore, and advanced close up to the buffalo. To inflict a wound thus in cool blood, I found a totally different thing from firing in the heat of the chase. Taking aim, however, just behind the fore-shoulder, my pistol for once proved true; the ball must have passed through the heart, for the animal gave one convulsive throe and expired.[3]

While I stood meditating and moralizing over the wreck I had so wantonly produced, with my horse grazing near me, I was rejoined by my fellow sportsman, the Virtuoso; who, being a man of universal adroitness, and withal, more experienced and hardened in the gentle art of "veneric," soon managed to carve out the tongue of the buffalo, and delivered it to me to bear back to the camp as a trophy.[4]

[3] "Mr. Irving had his short-lived hunting mania satisfied, as a ball from his gun brought down a second of the herd" (Latrobe, *Rambler*, I, 229).

[4] Extended accounts of this hunt were set down by both Ellsworth (*Narrative*, 120–24) and Latrobe (*Rambler*, I, 222–31).

A Comrade Lost.—A Search for the Camp.—The Commissioner, the Wild Horse, and the Buffalo.—A Wolf Serenade.

Oᴜʀ ꜱᴏʟɪᴄɪᴛᴜᴅᴇ was now awakened for the young Count. With his usual eagerness and impetuosity he had persisted in urging his jaded horse in pursuit of the herd, unwilling to return without having likewise killed a buffalo. In this way he had kept on following them, hither and thither, and occasionally firing an ineffectual shot, until by degrees horseman and herd became indistinct in the distance, and at length swelling ground and strips of trees and thickets hid them entirely from sight.

By the time my friend, the amateur,[1] joined me, the young Count had been long lost to view. We held a consultation on the matter. Evening was drawing on. Were we to pursue him, it would be dark before we should overtake him, granting we did not entirely lose trace of him in the gloom. We should then be too much bewildered to find our way back to the encampment; even now, our return would be difficult. We determined, therefore, to hasten to the camp as speedily as possible, and send out our half-breeds, and some of the veteran hunters, skilled in cruising about the prairies, to search for our companion.

We accordingly set forward in what we supposed to be the direction of the camp. Our weary horses could hardly be urged beyond a walk. The twilight thickened upon us; the landscape grew gradually indistinct; we tried in vain to recognize various landmarks which we had noted in the morning. The features of the prairies are so similar

[1] Latrobe. Irving used the word in its original sense.

as to baffle the eye of any but an Indian, or a practised woodman. At length night closed in. We hoped to see the distant glare of camp-fires; we listened to catch the sound of the bells about the necks of the grazing horses. Once or twice we thought we distinguished them; we were mistaken. Nothing was to be heard but a monotonous concert of insects, with now and then the dismal howl of wolves mingling with the night breeze. We began to think of halting for the night, and bivouacking under the lee of some thicket. We had implements to strike a light: there was plenty of firewood at hand, and the tongues of our buffaloes would furnish us with a repast.

Just as we were preparing to dismount, we heard the report of a rifle, and shortly after, the notes of the bugle, calling up the night guard. Pushing forward in that direction, the camp-fires soon broke on our sight, gleaming at a distance from among the thick groves of an alluvial bottom.

As we entered the camp, we found it a scene of rude hunters' revelry and wassail. There had been a grand day's sport, in which all had taken a part. Eight buffaloes had been killed; roaring fires were blazing on every side; all hands were feasting upon roasted joints, broiled marrow-bones, and the juicy hump, far-famed among the epicures of the prairies. Right glad were we to dismount and partake of the sturdy cheer, for we had been on our weary horses since morning without tasting food.

As to our worthy friend, the Commissioner, with whom we had parted company at the outset of this eventful day, we found him lying in a corner of the tent, much the worse for wear, in the course of a successful hunting match.[2]

2 "I was excessively tired, I had during the cold rains caught cold in my teeth and had a painful swelled face" (Ellsworth, *Narrative*, 123–24).

It seems that our man, Beatte, in his zeal to give the Commissioner an opportunity of distinguishing himself, and gratifying his hunting propensities, had mounted him upon his half-wild horse, and started him in pursuit of a huge buffalo bull, that had already been frightened by the hunters. The horse, which was fearless as his owner, and, like him, had a considerable spice of devil in his composition, and who, besides, had been made familiar with the game, no sooner came in sight and scent of the buffalo, than he set off full speed, bearing the involuntary hunter hither and thither, and whither he would not—up hill and down hill—leaping pools and brooks—dashing through glens and gullies, until he came up with the game. Instead of sheering off, he crowded upon the buffalo. The Commissioner, almost in self-defense, discharged both barrels of a double-barrelled gun into the enemy. The broadside took effect, but was not mortal. The buffalo turned furiously upon his pursuer: the horse, as he had been taught by his owner, wheeled off. The buffalo plunged after him. The worthy Commissioner, in great extremity, drew his sole pistol from his holster, fired it off as a stern-chaser, shot the buffalo full in the breast, and brought him lumbering forward to the earth.

The Commissioner returned to camp, lauded on all sides for his signal exploit; but grievously battered and way-worn. He had been a hard rider perforce, and a victor in spite of himself. He turned a deaf ear to all compliments and congratulations; had but little stomach for the hunter's fare placed before him, and soon retreated to stretch his limbs in the tent, declaring that nothing should tempt him again to mount that half devil Indian horse, and that he had enough of buffalo hunting for the rest of his life.[3]

It was too dark now to send anyone in search of the

[3] Compare Ellsworth's *Narrative*, 121–23.

young Count. Guns, however, were fired, and the bugles sounded from time to time, to guide him to the camp, if by chance he should straggle within hearing; but the night advanced without his making his appearance. There was not a star visible to guide him, and we concluded that wherever he was, he would give up wandering in the dark, and bivouac until daybreak.

It was a raw, overcast night. The carcasses of the buffaloes killed in the vicinity of the camp had drawn about it an unusual number of wolves, who kept up the most forlorn concert of whining yells, prolonged into dismal cadences and inflexions, literally converting the surrounding waste into a howling wilderness. Nothing is more melancholy than the midnight howl of a wolf on a prairie. What rendered the gloom and wildness of the night and the savage concert of the neighboring waste the more dreary to us, was the idea of the lonely and exposed situation of our young and inexperienced comrade. We trusted, however, that on the return of daylight, he would find his way back to the camp, and then all the events of the night would be remembered only as so many savory gratifications of his passion for adventure.

❧ XXXI ❧

A Hunt for a Lost Comrade.

THE MORNING DAWNED [October 30], and an hour or
two passed without any tidings of the Count. We began
to feel uneasiness lest, having no compass to aid him, he
might perplex himself and wander in some opposite direction. Stragglers are thus often lost for days; what made
us the more anxious about him was, that he had no provisions with him, was totally unversed in "woodcraft," and
liable to fall into the hands of some lurking or straggling
party of savages.

As soon as our people, therefore, had made their breakfast, we beat up for volunteers for a cruise in search of the
Count. A dozen of the rangers, mounted on some of the
best and freshest horses, and armed with rifles, were soon
ready to start; our half-breeds Beatte and Antoine also,
with our little mongrel Frenchman, were zealous in the
cause; so Mr. L. and myself taking the lead, to show the
way to the scene of our little hunt, where we had parted
company with the Count, we all set out across the prairie.
A ride of a couple of miles brought us to the carcasses of
the two buffaloes we had killed. A legion of ravenous
wolves were already gorging upon them. At our approach
they reluctantly drew off, skulking with a caitiff look to
the distance of a few hundred yards, and there awaiting
our departure, that they might return to their banquet.

I conducted Beatte and Antoine to the spot whence the
young Count had continued the chase alone. It was like
putting hounds upon the scent. They immediately dis-

tinguished the track of his horse amidst the tramplings of the buffaloes, and set off at a round pace, following with the eye in nearly a straight course, for upwards of a mile, when they came to where the herd had divided, and run hither and thither about a meadow. Here the track of the horse's hoofs wandered and doubled and often crossed each other; our half-breeds were like hounds at fault. While we were at a halt, waiting until they should unravel the maze, Beatte suddenly gave a short Indian whoop, or rather yelp, and pointed to a distant hill. On regarding it attentively, we perceived a horseman on the summit. "It is the Count!" cried Beatte, and set off at full gallop, followed by the whole company. In a few moments he checked his horse. Another figure on horseback had appeared on the brow of a hill. This completely altered the case. The Count had wandered off alone; no other person had been missing from the camp. If one of these horsemen were indeed the Count, the other must be an Indian. If an Indian, in all probability a Pawnee. Perhaps they were both Indians; scouts of some party lurking in the vicinity. While these and other suggestions were hastily discussed, the two horsemen glided down from the profile of the hill, and we lost sight of them. One of the rangers suggested that there might be a straggling party of Pawnees behind the hill, and the Count might have fallen into their hands. The idea had an electric effect upon the little troop. In an instant every horse was at full speed, the half-breeds leading the way; the young rangers as they rode set up wild yelps of exultation at the thoughts of having a brush with the Indians. A neck or nothing gallop brought us to the skirts of the hill, and revealed our mistake. In a ravine we found the two horsemen standing by the carcass of a buffalo which they had killed. They proved to be two rangers, who, unperceived, had left camp a little before us, and had come here in a direct line, while we had made a wide circuit about the prairie.

This episode being at an end, and the sudden excitement being over, we slowly and coolly retraced our steps to the meadow; but it was some time before our half-breeds could again get on the track of the Count. Having at length found it, they succeeded in following it through all its doublings, until they came to where it was no longer mingled with the tramp of buffaloes, but became single and separate, wandering here and there about the prairies, but always tending in a direction opposite to that of the camp. Here the Count had evidently given up the pursuit of the herd, and had endeavored to find his way to the encampment, but had become bewildered as the evening shades thickened around him, and had completely mistaken the points of the compass.

In all this quest our half-breeds displayed that quickness of eye, in following up a track, for which Indians are so noted. Beatte, especially, was as staunch as a veteran hound. Sometimes he would keep forward on an easy trot; his eyes fixed on the ground a little ahead of his horse, clearly distinguishing prints in the herbage which to me were invisible, excepting on the closest inspection. Sometimes he would pull up and walk his horse slowly, regarding the ground intensely, where to my eye nothing was apparent. Then he would dismount, lead his horse by the bridle, and advance cautiously step by step, with his face bent towards the earth, just catching, here and there, a casual indication of the vaguest kind to guide him onward. In some places where the soil was hard, and the grass withered, he would lose the track entirely, and wander backward and forward, and right and left, in search of it; returning occasionally to the place where he had lost sight of it, to take a new departure. If this failed he would examine the banks of the neighboring streams, or the sandy bottoms of the ravines, in hopes of finding tracks where the Count had crossed. When he again came upon the track, he would remount his horse, and resume his onward course. At length, after crossing a stream, in the crumbling banks of which the hoofs of the horse were deeply dented, we came upon a high dry prairie, where our half-breeds were completely baffled. Not a foot-print was to be discerned, though they searched in every direction; and Beatte, at length coming to a pause, shook his head despondingly.

Just then a small herd of deer, roused from a neighboring ravine, came bounding by us, Beatte sprang from his horse, levelled his rifle, and wounded one slightly, but without bringing it to the ground. The report of the rifle was almost immediately followed by a long halloo from a distance. We looked around, but could see nothing. Another long halloo was heard, and at length a horseman was descried, emerging out of a skirt of forest. A single glance showed him to be the young Count; there was a universal shout and scamper, every one setting off full gallop to greet him. It was a joyful meeting to both parties; for, much anxiety had been felt by us all on account of his youth and inexperience, and for his part, with all his love of adventure, he seemed right glad to be once more among his friends.

As we supposed he had completely mistaken his course on the preceding evening, and had wandered about until dark, when he thought of bivouacking. The night was cold, yet he feared to make a fire, lest it might betray him to some lurking party of Indians. Hobbling his horse with his pocket handkerchief, and leaving him to graze on the margin of the prairie, he clambered into a tree, fixed his saddle in the fork of the branches, and placing himself securely with his back against the trunk, prepared to pass a dreary and anxious night, regaled occasionally with the howlings of the wolves. He was agreeably disappointed. The fatigue of the day soon brought on a sound sleep; he had delightful dreams about his home in Switzerland, nor did he wake until it was broad daylight.

He then descended from his roosting-place, mounted his horse, and rode to the naked summit of a hill, whence he beheld a trackless wilderness around him, but at no great distance, the Grand Canadian, winding its way between borders of forest land.[1] The sight of this river consoled him with the idea that, should he fail in finding his way back to camp, or in being found by some party of his comrades, he might follow the course of the stream, which could not fail to conduct him to some frontier post, or Indian hamlet. So closed the events of our hap-hazard buffalo hunt.

[1] About three miles to the south, according to Latrobe (*Rambler*, I, 236).

⧫§ XXXII §⧫

A Republic of Prairie Dogs.

O N RETURNING from our expedition in quest of the young Count, I learned that a burrow, or village, as it is termed, of prairie dogs had been discovered on the level summit of a hill, about a mile from the camp.[1] Having heard much of the habits and peculiarities of these little animals, I determined to pay a visit to the community. The prairie dog is, in fact, one of the curiosities of the Far West, about which travellers delight to tell marvellous tales, endowing him at times with something of the politic and social habits of a rational being, and giving him systems of civil government and domestic economy, almost equal to what they used to bestow upon the beaver.

The prairie dog is an animal of the coney kind, and about the size of a rabbit.[2] He is of a sprightly mercurial nature; quick, sensitive, and somewhat petulant. He is very gregarious, living in large communities, sometimes of several acres in extent, where innumerable little heaps of earth show the entrances to the subterranean cells of the inhabitants, and the well beaten tracks, like lanes and streets, show their mobility and restlessness. According to the accounts given of them, they would seem to be continually full of sport, business, and public affairs; whisking about hither and thither, as if on gossiping visits to each other's

[1] Ellsworth visited this prairie dog village with Dr. Holt; he placed it three-quarters of a mile from camp (*Narrative*, 125–26). Latrobe also described it (*Rambler*, I, 236–38).

[2] Rodents, not rabbits.

houses, or congregating in the cool of the evening, or after a shower, and gambolling together in the open air. Sometimes, especially when the moon shines, they pass half the night in revelry, barking or yelping with short, quick, yet weak tones, like those of very young puppies. While in the height of their playfulness and clamor, however, should there be the least alarm, they all vanish into their cells in an instant, and the village remains blank and silent. In case they are hard pressed by their pursuers, without any hope of escape, they will assume a pugnacious air, and a most whimsical look of impotent wrath and defiance.

The prairie dogs are not permitted to remain sole and undisturbed inhabitants of their own homes. Owls and rattlesnakes are said to take up their abodes with them; but whether as invited guests or unwelcome intruders, is a matter of controversy. The owls are of a peculiar kind, and would seem to partake of the character of the hawk; for they are taller and more erect on their legs, more alert in their looks and rapid in their flight than ordinary owls, and do not confine their excursions to the night, but sally forth in broad day.

Some say that they only inhabit cells which the prairie dogs have deserted, and suffered to go to ruin, in consequence of the death in them of some relative; for they would make out this little animal to be endowed with keen sensibilities, that will not permit it to remain in the dwelling where it has witnessed the death of a friend. Other fanciful speculators represent the owl as a kind of housekeeper to the prairie dog; and, from having a note very similar, insinuate that it acts, in a manner, as family preceptor, and teaches the young litter to bark.

As to the rattlesnake, nothing satisfactory has been ascertained of the part he plays in this most interesting household; though he is considered as little better than a sycophant and sharper, that winds himself into the concerns of the honest, credulous little dog, and takes him in most sadly. Certain it is, if he acts as toad-eater, he occasionally solaces himself with more than the usual perquisites of his order; as he is now and then detected with one of the younger members of the family in his maw.

Such are a few of the particulars that I could gather about the domestic economy of this little inhabitant of the prairies, who, with his pigmy republic, appears to be a subject of much whimsical speculation and burlesque remarks, among the hunters of the Far West.

It was toward evening that I set out with a companion, to visit the village in question. Unluckily, it had been invaded in the course of the day by some of the rangers, who had shot two or three of its inhabitants, and thrown the whole sensitive community in confusion. As we approached, we could perceive numbers of the inhabitants seated at the entrances of their cells, while sentinels seemed to have been posted on the outskirts, to keep a look-out. At sight of us, the picket guards scampered in and gave the alarm; whereupon every inhabitant gave a short yelp, or bark, and dived into his hole, his heels twinkling in the air as if he had thrown a somerset.

We traversed the whole village, or republic, which covered an area of about thirty acres; but not a whisker of an inhabitant was to be seen. We probed their cells as far as the ramrods of our rifles would reach, but could unearth neither dog, nor owl, nor rattlesnake. Moving quietly to a little distance, we lay down upon the ground and watched for a long time, silent and motionless. By and by, a cautious old burgher would slowly put forth the end of his nose, but instantly draw it in again. Another, at a greater distance, would emerge entirely; but, catching a glance of us, would throw a somerset, and plunge back again into his hole. At length, some who resided on the opposite side of the village, taking courage from the continued stillness, would steal forth, and hurry off to a distant hole, the residence possibly of some family connection, or gossiping friend, about whose safety they were solicitous, or with whom they wished to compare notes about the late occurrences.

Others, still more bold, assembled in little knots, in the streets and public places, as if to discuss the recent outrages offered to the commonwealth, and the atrocious murders of their fellow-burghers.

We rose from the ground and moved forward, to take a nearer view of these public proceedings, when yelp! yelp! yelp!—there was a shrill alarm passed from mouth to mouth; the meetings suddenly dispersed; feet twinkled in the air in every direction; and in an instant all had vanished into the earth.[3]

The dusk of the evening put an end to our observations, but the train of whimsical comparisons produced in my brain by the moral attributes which I had heard given to these little politic animals, still continued after my return to camp; and late in the night, as I lay awake after all the camp was asleep, and heard in the stillness of the hour, a faint clamor of shrill voices from the distant village, I could not help picturing to myself the inhabitants gathered together in noisy assemblage and windy debate, to devise plans for the public safety, and to vindicate the invaded rights and insulted dignity of the republic.

[3] At the close of the second extant notebook (September 26–October 6), Irving entered a few notes about prairie dogs (*Western Journals*, 104–105).

⤳ XXXIII ⤳

*A Council in the Camp.—Reasons for Facing Homeward.
—Horses Lost.—Departure with a Detachment on the
Homeward Route.—Swamp.—Wild Horse.—Camp Scene
by Night.—The Owl, Harbinger of Dawn.*

W HILE BREAKFAST was preparing [October 31], a
council was held as to our future movements. Symptoms
of discontent had appeared for a day or two past among
the rangers, most of whom, unaccustomed to the life of the
prairies, had become impatient of its privations, as well as
the restraints of the camp. The want of bread had been
felt severely, and they were wearied with constant travel.
In fact, the novelty and excitement of the expedition were
at an end. They had hunted the deer, the bear, the elk,
the buffalo, and the wild horse, and had no further object
of leading interest to look forward to. A general inclination prevailed, therefore, to turn homeward.[1]

Grave reasons disposed the Captain and his officers to
adopt this resolution. Our horses were generally much
jaded by the fatigues of travelling and hunting, and had
fallen away sadly for want of good pasturage, and from

[1] Though he says nothing of it, Irving himself may have been
willing to turn back. On October 30, Ellsworth wrote: "Mr Irving
has been much afflicted for several days with a breaking out on the
wri[s]ts & face—indeed the scorbutic affection seems to extend over
the whole body—I have attributed it to his meat diet, but he thinks
it arises from some other cause—Whatever the cause—the irritation
gives him much pain and makes him so restless that he cannot sleep—
I pitied him many nights—the only relief he could get, was to wash
himself in a weak solution of salt water—He thought he should
find much relief if he could get into sheets, for blankets were un-
comfortable to him—but sheets are not the soldiers fare" (*Narrative*,
128). In his journal, Irving noted the arrest, on the evening of October 30, of a corporal for mutinous talk (*Western Journals*, 139).

being tethered at night, to protect them from Indian depredations. The late rains, too, seemed to have washed away the nourishment from the scanty herbage that remained; and since our encampment during the storm, our horses had lost flesh and strength rapidly. With every possible care, horses, accustomed to grain, and to the regular and plentiful nourishment of the stable and the farm, lose heart and condition in travelling on the prairies. In all expeditions of the kind we were engaged in, the hardy Indian horses, which are generally mustangs, or a cross of the wild breed, are to be preferred. They can stand all fatigues, hardships, and privations, and thrive on the grasses and the wild herbage of the plains.

Our men, too, had acted with little forethought; galloping off whenever they had a chance, after the game that we encountered while on the march. In this way they had strained and wearied their horses, instead of husbanding their strength and spirits. On a tour of the kind, horses should as seldom as possible be put off of a quiet walk; and the average day's journey should not exceed ten miles.

We had hoped, by pushing forward, to reach the bottoms of the Red River, which abound with young cane, a most nourishing forage for cattle at this season of the year. It would now take us several days to arrive there, and in the meantime many of our horses would probably give out. It was the time, too, when the hunting parties of Indians set fire to the prairies; the herbage, throughout this part of the country, was in that parched state, favorable to combustion, and there was daily more and more risk, that the prairies between us and the fort would be set on fire by some of the return parties of Osages, and a scorched desert left for us to traverse. In a word, we had started too late in the season, or loitered too much in the early part of our march, to accomplish our originally-intended tour; and there was imminent hazard, if we continued on, that we should lose the greater part of our horses; and, besides suffering various other inconveniences, be obliged to return on foot. It was determined, therefore, to give up all further progress, and, turning our faces to the southeast,[2] to make the best of our way back to Fort Gibson.

This resolution being taken, there was an immediate eagerness to put it into operation. Several horses, however, were missing, and among others those of the Captain and the Surgeon. Persons had gone in search of them, but the morning advanced without any tidings of them. Our party, in the meantime, being all ready for a march, the Commissioner determined to set off in the advance, with his original escort of a lieutenant and fourteen rangers, leaving the Captain to come on at his convenience, with the main body.[3] At ten o'clock we accordingly started, under the guidance of Beatte, who had hunted over this part of the country, and knew the direct route to the garrison.

For some distance we skirted the prairie, keeping a southeast direction; and in the course of our ride we saw a variety of wild animals, deer, white and black wolves, buffaloes, and wild horses. To the latter, our half-breeds and Tonish gave ineffectual chase, only serving to add to the weariness of their already jaded steeds. Indeed it is rarely that any but the weaker and least fleet of the wild horses are taken in these hard racings; while the horse of the huntsman is prone to be knocked up. The latter, in

[2] Their direction home would have to be northeast, but they began the return by moving southeast over the open prairie, along the bank of the Canadian.

[3] Pentecost and twenty men, according to Ellsworth (*Narrative*, 129).

fact, risks a good horse to catch a bad one. On this occasion, Tonish, who was a perfect imp on horseback, and noted for ruining every animal he bestrode, succeeded in laming and almost disabling the powerful gray on which we had mounted him at the outset of our tour.

After proceeding a few miles, we left the prairie, and struck to the east, taking what Beatte pronounced an old Osage war-track. This led us through a rugged tract of country, overgrown with scrubbed forests and entangled thickets and intersected by deep ravines, and brisk-running streams, the sources of Little River.[4] About three o'clock, we encamped by some pools of water in a small valley, having come about fourteen miles. We had brought on a supply of provisions from our last camp, and supped heartily upon stewed buffalo meat, roasted venison, beignets, or fritters of flour fried in bear's lard, and tea made of a species of the goldenrod, which we had found, throughout our whole route, almost as grateful a beverage as coffee.[5] Indeed our coffee, which, as long as it held out, had been served up with every meal, according to the custom of the West, was by no means a beverage to boast of. It was roasted in a frying-pan, without much care, pounded in a leathern bag, with a round stone, and boiled in our prime and almost only kitchen utensil, the camp-kettle, in "branch" or brook water; which, on the prairies, is deeply

[4] More Cross Timbers (Ellsworth, *Narrative*, 131). Latrobe wrote briefly with some feeling: "The greater part of the first four [days' march] we were employed in breaking a painful pathway with many a tear, scratch, and grumble, through the Cross Timbers" (*Rambler*, I, 239).

[5] Ellsworth had first mentioned this "prairie tea" soon after they left Fort Gibson; Tonish had pointed it out to him. "—it is *sudorific, gently stimulating* and an active diuretic—in large quantities it is laxative—Mr Irving is so much pleased with it, that he has ordered a quantity for New York" (*Narrative*, 17).

colored by the soil, of which it always holds abundant particles in a state of solution and suspension. In fact, in the course of our tour, we had tasted the quality of every variety of soil, and the draughts of water we had taken might vie in diversity of color, if not of flavor, with the tinctures of an apothecary's shop. Pure, limpid water is a rare luxury on the prairies, at least at this season of the year. Supper over, we placed sentinels about our scanty and diminished camp, spread our skins and blankets under the trees, now nearly destitute of foliage, and slept soundly until morning.

We had a beautiful daybreak [November 1]. The camp again resounded with cheerful voices; every one was animated with the thoughts of soon being at the fort, and revelling on bread and vegetables. Even our saturnine man, Beatte, seemed inspired on this occasion; and as he drove up the horses for the march, I heard him singing, in nasal tones, a most forlorn Indian ditty. All this transient gayety, however, soon died away amidst the fatigues of our march, which lay through the same kind of rough, hilly, thicketed country as that of yesterday. In the course of the morning we arrived at the valley of the Little River, where it wound through a broad bottom of alluvial soil. At present it had overflowed its banks, and inundated a great part of the valley. The difficulty was to distinguish the stream from the broad sheets of water it had formed, and to find a place where it might be forded; for it was in general deep and miry, with abrupt crumbling banks. Under the pilotage of Beatte, therefore, we wandered for some time among the links made by this winding stream, in what appeared to us as a trackless labyrinth of swamps, thickets, and standing pools. Sometimes our jaded horses dragged their limbs forward with the utmost difficulty, having to toil for a great distance, with the water up to the stirrups, and beset at the bottom with roots and creeping plants. Sometimes we had to force our way through dense thickets of brambles and grapevines, which almost pulled us out of our saddles. In one place, one of the pack-horses sunk in the mire and fell on his side, so as to be extricated with great difficulty. Wherever the soil was bare, or there was a sand-bank, we beheld innumerable tracks of bears, wolves, wild horses, turkeys, and water-fowl; showing the abundant sport this valley might afford to the huntsman. Our men, however, were sated with hunting, and too weary to be excited by these signs, which in the outset of our tour would have put them in a fever of anticipation. Their only desire, at present, was to push on doggedly for the fortress.

At length we succeeded in finding a fording place, where we all crossed Little River, with the water and mire to the saddle-girths, and then halted for an hour and a half, to overhaul the wet baggage, and give the horses time to rest.[6]

On resuming our march, we came to a pleasant little meadow, surrounded by groves of elms and cotton-wood trees, in the midst of which was a fine black horse grazing. Beatte, who was in advance, beckoned us to halt, and, being mounted on a mare, approached the horse gently, step by step, imitating the whinny of the animal with admirable exactness. The noble courser of the prairie gazed for a time, snuffed the air, neighed, pricked up his ears, pranced round and round the mare in gallant style; but kept at too great a distance for Beatte to throw the lariat.

[6] Ellsworth too described the difficulties of crossing the Grand Bayou or Little River (*Narrative*, 134–35). During the noon rest, Irving hung up to dry "the two shirts which I washed yesterday" (*Western Journals*, 142).

He was a magnificent object, in all the pride and glory of his nature. It was admirable to see the lofty and airy carriage of his head; the freedom of every movement; the elasticity with which he trod the meadow. Finding it impossible to get within noosing distance, and seeing that the horse was receding and growing alarmed, Beatte slid down from his saddle, levelled his rifle across the back of his mare, and took aim, with the evident intention of creasing him. I felt a throb of anxiety for the safety of the noble animal, and called out to Beatte to desist. It was too late; he pulled the trigger as I spoke; luckily he did not shoot with his usual accuracy, and I had the satisfaction to see the coal-black steed dash off unharmed into the forest.

On leaving this valley, we ascended among broken hills and rugged, ragged forests, equally harassing to horse and rider. The ravines, too, were of red clay, and often so steep that, in descending, the horses would put their feet together and fairly slide down, and then scramble up the opposite side like cats. Here and there, among the thickets in the valleys, we met with sloes and persimmon, and the eagerness with which our men broke from the line of march, and ran to gather these poor fruits, showed how much they craved some vegetable condiment, after living so long exclusively on animal food.

About half past three we encamped near a brook in a meadow where there was some scanty herbage for our half-famished horses. As Beatte had killed a fat doe in the course of the day, and one of our company a fine turkey, we did not lack for provisions.

It was a splendid autumnal evening. The horizon, after sunset, was of a clear apple green, rising into a delicate lake which gradually lost itself in a deep purple blue. One narrow streak of cloud, of a mahogany color, edged with amber and gold, floated in the west, and just beneath it was the evening star, shining with the pure brilliancy of a diamond. In unison with this scene, there was an evening concert of insects of various kinds, all blended and harmonized into one sober and somewhat melancholy note, which I have always found to have a soothing effect upon the mind, disposing it to quiet musings.

The night that succeeded was calm and beautiful. There was a faint light from the moon, now in its second quarter, and after it had set, a fine starlight, with shooting meteors. The wearied rangers, after a little murmuring conversation round their fires, sank to rest at an early hour, and I seemed to have the whole scene to myself. It is delightful, in thus bivouacking on the prairies, to lie awake and gaze at the stars; it is like watching them from the deck of a ship at sea, when at one view we have the whole cope of heaven. One realizes, in such lonely scenes, that companionship with these beautiful luminaries which made astronomers of the eastern shepherds, as they watched their flocks by night. How often, while contemplating their mild and benignant radiance, I have called to mind the exquisite text of Job: "Canst thou bind the secret influences of the Pleiades, or loose the bands of Orion?"[7] I do not know why it was, but I felt this night unusually affected by the solemn magnificence of the firmament; and seemed, as I lay thus under the open vault of heaven, to inhale with the pure untainted air, an exhilarating buoyancy of spirit, and, as it were, an ecstacy of mind. I slept and waked alternately; and when I slept, my dreams partook of the happy tone of my waking reveries. Toward morning, one of the sentinels, the oldest man in the troop, came and took a seat near me; he was weary and sleepy, and impatient to be relieved.[8]

[7] Job 38:31. The quotation should have read: "Canst thou bind the sweet influences of Pleiades, or loose the bands of Orion?"

I found he had been gazing at the heavens also, but with different feelings.

"If the stars don't deceive me," said he, "it is near day-break."

"There can be no doubt of that," said Beatte, who lay close by. "I heard an owl just now."

"Does the owl, then, hoot toward daybreak?" asked I.

"Aye, sir, just as the cock crows."

This was a useful habitude of the bird of wisdom, of which I was not aware. Neither the stars nor owl deceived their votaries. In a short time there was a faint streak of light in the east.

[8] According to the journal, it was on the evening of the thirty-first that "Old Mr Sawyer sits at foot of my bed & gossips until I fall asleep" (*Western Journals*, 141).

Old Creek Encampment.—Scarcity of Provisions.—Bad Weather.—Weary Marching.—A Hunter's Bridge.

THE COUNTRY through which we passed this morning (Nov. 2), was less rugged, and of more agreeable aspect than that we had lately traversed. At eleven o'clock, we came out upon an extensive prairie, and about six miles to our left beheld a long line of green forest, marking the course of the north fork of the Arkansas.[1] On the edge of the prairie, and in a spacious grove of noble trees which overshadowed a small brook, were the traces of an old Creek hunting camp. On the bark of the trees were rude delineations of hunters and squaws, scrawled with charcoal; together with various signs and hieroglyphics, which our half-breeds interpreted as indicating that from this encampment the hunters had returned home.[2]

In this beautiful camping ground we made our mid-day halt. While reposing under the trees, we heard a shouting at no great distance, and presently the Captain and the main body of rangers, whom we had left behind two days since, emerged from the thickets, and crossing the brook, were joyfully welcomed into the camp. The Captain and

[1] *Sic*. It is, of course, a slip for the "Canadian."

[2] There is no entry in Irving's journal for November 2. He has here toned down the picture, for Ellsworth wrote of it: "The Creek Indians have a *very indecent* manner of making pictures on the trees. The wood is first cut off, and with paints they represent the warrior in such attitudes of amorous feeling in going or returning as may be indicative of their true sensations, but very abhorrent to every principle of modesty or virtue—I forbear giving details—" (*Narrative*, 136).

the Doctor had been unsuccessful in the search after their horses, and were obliged to march for the greater part of the time on foot; yet they had come on with more than ordinary speed.

We resumed our march about one o'clock, keeping easterly, and approaching the north fork obliquely; it was late before we found a good camping-place; the beds of the streams were dry, the prairies, too, had been burnt in various places, by Indian hunting parties. At length we found water in a small alluvial bottom, where there was tolerable pasturage.

On the following morning [November 3], there were flashes of lightning in the east, with low, rumbling thunder, and clouds began to gather about the horizon. Beatte prognosticated rain, and that the wind would veer to the north. In the course of our march, a flock of brant were seen overhead, flying from the north. "There comes the wind!" said Beatte; and, in fact, it began to blow from that quarter almost immediately, with occasional flurries of rain. About half past nine o'clock, we forded the north fork of the Canadian, and encamped about one, that our hunters might have time to beat up the neighborhood for game; for a serious scarcity began to prevail in the camp. Most of the rangers were young, heedless, and inexperienced, and could not be prevailed upon, while provisions abounded, to provide for the future, by jerking meat, or carry away any on their horses. On leaving an encampment, they would leave quantities of meat lying about, trusting to Providence and their rifles for a future supply. The consequence was, that any temporary scarcity of game, or ill luck in hunting, produced almost a famine in the camp. In the present instance, they had left loads of buffalo meat at the camp on the great prairie; and, having ever since been on a forced march, leaving no time for hunting, they were now destitute of supplies, and pinched with hunger. Some had not eaten anything since the morning of the preceding day. Nothing would have persuaded them, when revelling in the abundance of the buffalo encampment, that they would so soon be in such famishing plight.

The hunters returned with indifferent success. The game had been frightened away from this part of the country by Indian hunting parties, which had preceded us. Ten or a dozen wild turkeys were brought in, but not a deer had been seen. The rangers began to think turkeys and even prairie hens deserving of attention; game which they had hitherto considered unworthy of their rifles.

The night was cold and windy, with occasional sprinklings of rain; but we had roaring fires to keep us comfortable. In the night, a flight of wild geese passed over the camp, making a great cackling in the air; symptoms of approaching winter.

We set forward at an early hour the next morning, in a northeast course, and came upon the trace of a party of Creek Indians, which enabled our poor horses to travel with more ease. We entered upon a fine champaign country. From a rising ground we had a noble prospect, over extensive prairies, finely diversified by groves and tracts of woodland, and bounded by long lines of distant hills, all clothed with the rich mellow tints of autumn. Game, too, was more plenty. A fine buck sprang up from among the herbage on our right, and dashed off at full speed; but a young ranger by the name of Childers,[3] who was on foot, levelled his rifle, discharged a ball that broke the neck of the bounding deer, and sent him tumbling head over heels forward. Another buck and a doe, besides several turkeys, were killed before we came to a halt, so that

[3] Alexander C. Childers of Batesville was a bugler (*Western Journals*, 182).

the hungry mouths of the troop were once more supplied.[4]

About three o'clock we encamped in a grove after a forced march of twenty-five miles, that had proved a hard trial to the horses. For a long time after the head of the line had encamped, the rest kept straggling in, two and three at a time; one of our pack-horses had given out, about nine miles back, and a pony belonging to Beatte, shortly after. Many of the other horses looked so gaunt and feeble, that doubts were entertained of their being able to reach the fort. In the night there was heavy rain, and the morning dawned cloudy and dismal. The camp resounded, however, with something of its former gayety.[5] The rangers had supped well, and were renovated in spirits, anticipating a speedy arrival at the garrison. Before we set forward on our march, Beatte returned, and brought his pony to the camp with great difficulty. The pack-horse, however, was completely knocked up and had to be abandoned.[6] The wild mare, too, had cast her foal, through exhaustion, and was not in a state to go forward. She and the pony, therefore, were left at this encampment, where there was water and good pasturage; and where there would be a chance of their reviving, and being afterward sought out and brought to the garrison.

We set off about eight o'clock [November 5], and had a day of weary and harassing travel; part of the time over rough hills, and part over rolling prairies. The rain had rendered the soil slippery and plashy, so as to afford un-

[4] Although Irving does not mention it here, in his journal he credited Tonish with a much-welcomed doe (*Western Journals*, 145). Latrobe and Ellsworth also record this.

[5] "Camp before daylight—sounds with imitation of cock crowing—owls hooting—the poor fellows had supper last night and are cheerful again" (*Western Journals*, 145).

[6] Old Gumbo (*Western Journals*, 145).

steady foothold. Some of the rangers dismounted, their horses having no longer strength to bear them. We made a halt in the course of the morning, but the horses were too tired to graze. Several of them lay down, and there was some difficulty in getting them on their feet again. Our troop presented a forlorn appearance[7] straggling slowly along, in a broken and scattered line, that extended over hill and dale, for three miles and upward, in groups of three and four, widely apart; some on horseback, some on foot, with a few laggards far in the rear. About four o'clock, we halted for the night in a spacious forest, beside a deep narrow river, called the Little North Fork, or Deep Creek.[8] It was late before the main part of the troop straggled into the encampment, many of the horses having given out. As this stream was too deep to be forded, we waited until the next day to devise means to cross it; but our half-breeds swam the horses of our party to the other side in the evening, as they would have better pasturage, and the stream was evidently swelling. The night was cold and unruly; the wind sounding hoarsely through the forest and whirling about the dry leaves. We made long fires of great trunks of trees, which diffused something of consolation if not cheerfulness around.

[7] "As to our personal appearance . . . our wardrobe had reached the lowest degree of poverty. . . . The Commissioner's dignity was completely shrouded in a common soldier's great-coat and pantaloons. Mr. Irving was clad in a suit of shirt armour, or to speak plainly, wore a strong holland shirt over his surtout; and one tail of the latter had been left in the embraces of the Cross Timbers. Certain of Pourtalès' integuments fluttered in the wind; and as to myself, though cased in buck-skin from head to foot, there were too many signs of wear and tear in my vestments to allow me any degree of self-congratulations over my fellows" (Latrobe, *Rambler*, I, 241).

[8] The Deep Fork, which enters the North Fork not far above the merge of the latter stream with the Canadian.

The next morning [November 6] there was general permission given to hunt until twelve o'clock; the camp being destitute of provisions. The rich woody bottom in which we were encamped abounded with wild turkeys, of which a considerable number were killed. In the meantime, preparations were made for crossing the river, which had risen several feet during the night; and it was determined to fell trees for the purpose, to serve as bridges.

The Captain and Doctor, and one or two other leaders of the camp, versed in woodcraft, examined, with learned eye, the trees growing on the river bank, until they singled out a couple of the largest size, and most suitable inclination. The axe was then vigorously applied to their roots, in such a way as to insure their falling directly across the stream. As they did not reach to the opposite bank, it was necessary for some of the men to swim across and fell trees on the other side, to meet them. They at length succeeded in making a precarious footway across the deep and rapid current, by which the baggage could be carried over; but it was necessary to grope our way, step by step, along the trunks and main branches of the trees, which for a part of the distance were completely submerged, so that we were to our waists in water.[9] Most of the horses were then swam across, but some of them were too weak to brave the current, and evidently too much knocked up to bear any further travel. Twelve men, therefore, were left at the encampment to guard these horses, until, by repose and good pasturage, they should be sufficiently recovered to complete their journey; and the Captain engaged to send the men a supply of flour and other necessaries, as soon as we should arrive at the fort.

[9] "Mr. Ellsworth & I pass across felled tree, holding by a stretched cord & aided by Billet" (*Western Journals,* 147). See also Ellsworth, *Narrative,* 139–40.

ᦉᦉ XXXV ᦉᦉ

A Look-out for Land.—Hard Travelling and Hungry Halting.—A Frontier Farm-House.—Arrival at the Garrison.

It was a little after one o'clock when we again resumed our weary wayfaring. The residue of that day and the whole of the next [November 7] were spent in toilsome travel. Part of the way was over stony hills, part across wide prairies, rendered spongy and miry by the recent rain, and cut up by brooks swollen into torrents. Our poor horses were so feeble, that it was with difficulty we could get them across the deep ravines and turbulent streams. In traversing the miry plains, they slipped and staggered at every step, and most of us were obliged to dismount and walk for the greater part of the way. Hunger prevailed throughout the troop; every one began to look anxious and haggard, and to feel the growing length of each additional mile. At one time, in crossing a hill, Beatte climbed a high tree, commanding a wide prospect, and took a look-out, like a mariner from the mast-head at sea. He came down with cheering tidings. To the left he had beheld a line of forest stretching across the country, which he knew to be the woody border of the Arkansas; and at a distance he had recognized certain landmarks, from which he concluded that we could not be above forty miles distant from the fort. It was like the welcome cry of land to tempest-tossed mariners.[1]

In fact we soon after saw smoke rising from a woody

[1] According to Irving's journal, Beatte so sighted the Arkansas on November 6 (*Western Journals*, 148). At this time they were close to the site of present-day Okmulgee.

glen at a distance. It was supposed to be made by a hunting party of Creek or Osage Indians from the neighborhood of the fort, and was joyfully hailed as a harbinger of man. It was now confidently hoped that we would soon arrive among the frontier hamlets of Creek Indians, which are scattered along the skirts of the uninhabited wilderness; and our hungry rangers trudged forward with reviving spirit, regaling themselves with savory anticipations of farm-house luxuries, and enumerating every article of good cheer, until their mouths fairly watered at the shadowy feasts thus conjured up.

A hungry night, however, closed in upon a toilsome day. We encamped on the border of one of the tributary streams of the Arkansas, amidst the ruins of a stately grove that had been riven by a hurricane.[2] The blast had torn its way through the forest in a narrow column, and its course was marked by enormous trees shivered and splintered, and upturned, with their roots in the air: all lay in one direction, like so many brittle reeds broken and trodden down by the hunter.

Here was fuel in abundance, without the labor of the axe; we had soon immense fires blazing and sparkling in the frosty air, and lighting up the whole forest; but, alas! we had no meat to cook at them. The scarcity in the camp almost amounted to famine. Happy was he who had a morsel of jerked meat, or even the half-picked bones of a former repast. For our part, we were more lucky at our mess than our neighbors; one of our men having shot a turkey. We had no bread to eat with it, nor salt to season it withal. It was simply boiled in water; the latter was served up as soup, and we were fain to rub each morsel of the turkey on the empty salt-bag, in hopes some saline particle might remain to relieve its insipidity.

[2] Pecan Creek enters the Arkansas about ten miles above the Verdigris River.

A Tour on the Prairies

The night was biting cold; the brilliant moonlight
sparkled on the frosty crystals which covered every object
around us. The water froze beside the skins on which we
bivouacked, and in the morning I found the blanket in
which I was wrapped covered with a hoar frost; yet I had
never slept more comfortably.

After a shadow of a breakfast [November 8], consisting
of turkey bones and a cup of coffee without sugar, we de-
camped at an early hour; for hunger is a sharp quickener
on a journey. The prairies were all gemmed with frost,
that covered the tall weeds and glistened in the sun. We
saw great flights of prairie hens, or grouse, that hovered
from tree to tree, or sat in rows along the naked branches,
waiting until the sun should melt the frost from the weeds
and herbage. Our rangers no longer despised such humble
game, but turned from the ranks in pursuit of a prairie hen
as eagerly as they formerly would go in pursuit of a deer.

Every one now pushed forward, anxious to arrive at
some human habitation before night. The poor horses were
urged beyond their strength, in the thought of soon being
able to indemnify them for present toil, by rest and ample
provender. Still the distances seemed to stretch out more
than ever, and the blue hills, pointed out as landmarks on
the horizon, to recede as we advanced. Every step became
a labor; every now and then a miserable horse would give
out and lie down. His owner would raise him by main
strength, force him forward to the margin of some stream,
where there might be a scanty border of herbage, and
then abandon him to his fate. Among those that were thus
left on the way, was one of the led horses of the Count;
a prime hunter, that had taken the lead of every thing in
the chase of the wild horses. It was intended, however, as
soon as we should arrive at the fort, to send out a party
provided with corn, to bring in such of the horses as should
survive.

In the course of the morning we came upon Indian tracks, crossing each other in various directions, a proof that we must be in the neighborhood of human habitations. At length, on passing through a skirt of wood, we beheld two or three log houses, sheltered under lofty trees on the border of a prairie, the habitations of Creek Indians, who had small farms adjacent. Had they been sumptuous villas, abounding with the luxuries of civilization, they could not have been hailed with greater delight.[3]

Some of the rangers rode up to them in quest of food: the greater part, however, pushed forward in search of the habitation of a white settler, which we were told was at no great distance. The troop soon disappeared among the trees, and I followed slowly in their track; for my once fleet and generous steed faltered under me, and was just able to drag one foot after the other, yet I was too weary and exhausted to spare him.[4]

In this way we crept on, until, on turning a thick clump of trees, a frontier farm-house suddenly presented itself to view.[5] It was a low tenement of logs, overshadowed by great forest trees, but it seemed as if a very region of Cocaigne prevailed around it. Here was a stable and barn, and granaries teeming with abundance, while legions of grunting swine, gobbling turkeys, cackling hens and strutting roosters swarmed about the farm-yard.

My poor jaded and half-famished horse raised his head and pricked up his ears at the well-known sights and sounds. He gave a chuckling inward sound, something like a dry laugh; whisked his tail, and made great leeway toward a corn-crib, filled with golden ears of maize, and it was

[3] They did not, however, stop there.

[4] According to Ellsworth, both he and Irving were walking most of the time on November 7 and 8 (*Narrative*, 143).

[5] Two miles beyond the Creek cabins (Ellsworth, *Narrative*, 142).

with some difficulty that I could control his course, and
steer him up to the door of the cabin. A single glance
within was sufficient to raise every gastronomic faculty.
There sat the Captain of the rangers and his officers, round
a three-legged table, crowned by a broad and smoking
dish of boiled beef and turnips. I sprang off my horse in an
instant, cast him loose to make his way to the corn-crib,
and entered this palace of plenty. A fat good-humored
negress received me at the door. She was the mistress of
the house, the spouse of the white man, who was absent.
I hailed her as some swart fairy of the wild, that had suddenly conjured up a banquet in the desert; and a banquet
was it in good sooth. In a twinkling, she lugged from the
fire a huge iron pot, that might have rivalled one of the
famous flesh-pots of Egypt, or the witches' caldron in
Macbeth. Placing a brown earthen dish on the floor, she
inclined the corpulent caldron on one side, and out leaped
sundry great morsels of beef, with a regiment of turnips
tumbling after them, and a rich cascade of broth overflowing the whole. This she handed me with an ivory smile that
extended from ear to ear; apologizing for our humble fare,
and the humble style in which it was served up. Humble
fare! humble style! Boiled beef and turnips, and an earthen
dish to eat them from! To think of apologizing for such
a treat to a half-starved man from the prairies; and then
such magnificent slices of bread and butter! Head of Api-
cius, what a banquet![6]

"The rage of hunger" being appeased, I began to think

[6] Bradley's. "Delightful sight of hogs" Irving noted in his journal
as he approached this cabin (*Western Journals*, 149). "I never eat
faster or more to my satisfaction," wrote Ellsworth. "Mr Irving
relished the meal quite as much as I did and will have a good story
to tell in his sketch book about Madame Bradleys entertainment"
(*Narrative*, 143).

of my horse. He, however, like an old campaigner, had taken good care of himself. I found him paying assiduous attention to the crib of Indian corn, and dexterously drawing forth and munching the ears that protruded between the bars. It was with great regret that I interrupted his repast, which he abandoned with a heavy sigh, or rather a rumbling groan. I was anxious, however, to rejoin my travelling companions, who had passed by the farm-house without stopping, and proceeded to the banks of the Arkansas; being in hopes of arriving before night at the Osage Agency. Leaving the Captain and his troop, therefore, amidst the abundance of the farm, where they had determined to quarter themselves for the night, I bade adieu to our sable hostess, and again pushed forward.[7]

A ride of about a mile brought me to where my comrades were waiting on the banks of the Arkansas, which here poured along between beautiful forests.[8] A number of Creek Indians, in their brightly colored dresses, looking like so many gay tropical birds, were busy aiding our men to transport the baggage across the river in a canoe. While this was doing, our horses had another regale from two great cribs heaped up with ears of Indian corn, which stood near the edge of the river. We had to keep a check upon the poor half-famished animals, lest they should injure themselves by their voracity.

The baggage being all carried to the opposite bank, we embarked in the canoe, and swam our horses across the river. I was fearful, lest in their enfeebled state, they should

[7] Ellsworth wrote that Antoine interrupted their meal to urge them to hurry if they were to get across the Arkansas to Colonel Chouteau's that night (*Narrative*, 143).

[8] They had hurried at a walk according to Ellsworth: "Mr Irving would not mount his tired horse" (*Narrative*, 143). The Commissioner gave the distance as two miles.

not be able to stem the current; but their banquet of Indian corn had already infused fresh life and spirit into them, and it would appear as if they were cheered by the instinctive consciousness of their approach to home, where they would soon be at rest, and in plentiful quarters; for no sooner had we landed and resumed our route, than they set off on a hand-gallop, and continued so for a great part of seven miles, that we had to ride through the woods.

It was an early hour in the evening when we arrived at the Agency, on the banks of the Verdigris River, whence we had set off about a month before.[9] Here we passed the night comfortably quartered; yet, after having been accustomed to sleep in the open air, the confinement of a chamber was, in some respects, irksome. The atmosphere seemed close, and destitute of freshness; and when I woke in the night and gazed about me upon complete darkness, I missed the glorious companionship of the stars.[10]

The next morning, after breakfast, I again set forward, in company with the worthy Commissioner, for Fort Gibson, where we arrived much tattered, travel-stained, and weather-beaten, but in high health and spirits;—and thus ended my foray into the Pawnee Hunting Grounds.[11]

[9] They arrived at Colonel Chouteau's trading post (which Irving called the Osage Agency) in time for supper (*Western Journals*, 150; Ellsworth, *Narrative*, 144).

[10] "We staid at Col Chouteaus store in a small room, with a large fire—a Mr Dudding & a young Doct. took one bed and the other was left for Mr Irving & myself—but we never *bundled* so some blanketts were spread, upon the floor for *him* as he insisted upon the Lord Commissioner taking the bed—our rest was very poor— both were too hot—and we longed for morning which came slowly along" (*Narrative*, 144–45).

[11] Irving had expected to stay at the fort for eight or ten days, but a steamboat leaving on November 10 provided an opportunity too good to miss (*Western Journals*, 151; Ellsworth, *Narrative*, 145).